THE POLAR REGIONS

OR,
A SEARCH AFTER
SIR JOHN FRANKLIN'S EXPEDITION

By

SHERARD OSBORN

First published in 1854

Read & Co.

This edition is published by Read & Co. History,
an imprint of Read & Co.

British Library Cataloguing-in-Publication Data
A catalogue record for this book is available
from the British Library.

Read & Co. is part of Read Books Ltd.
For more information visit
www.readandcobooks.co.uk

SIR JOHN FRANKLIN

By John Knox Laughton

Arctic explorer, the twelfth and youngest son of Willingham Franklin of Spilsby in Lincolnshire, was born on 16 April 1786. It had been intended to bring him up for the church, but a holiday visit to the seashore excited a strong desire to go to sea, which his father vainly endeavoured to overcome by sending him for a voyage in a merchant vessel as far as Lisbon. On his return he entered the royal navy on board the Polyphemus, then just sailing for the Baltic, where she played a leading part in the battle of Copenhagen. Two months later Franklin was appointed as a midshipman to the Investigator, under the command of his cousin, Matthew Flinders, and on the point of sailing for Australia. While in the Investigator Franklin distinguished himself by his remarkable aptitude for nautical and astronomical observations; he was employed at Sydney as assistant in a little observatory which Flinders established, and won the notice of Captain King, the governor, who used to address him familiarly as Mr. Tycho Brahe. When the ship's company was broken up after the wreck of the Porpoise, Franklin accompanied Lieutenant Fowler to China in the Rolla, and, taking a passage home in the East India Company's ship Earl Camden, was with Commodore Dance in his extraordinary engagement with Linois (15 Feb. 1804), on which occasion Fowler commanded on the lower deck and Franklin took charge of the signals. On arriving in England Franklin was appointed to the Bellerophon, in which he was present in the battle of Trafalgar, again having charge of the signals, and being one of the few on the Bellerophon's poop who escaped unhurt. Two years later he joined the Bedford, and, continuing in her after his promotion to lieutenant's rank (11 Feb. 1808), was employed on the home station till the peace in 1814, when the ship was ordered to North America, to form part of the expedition against New Orleans. In a boat attack on some gunboats in Lac Borgne Franklin was slightly wounded; and he had besides a full share in the laborious duties of the campaign. Its failure may account for the fact that no attention was paid to the strong recommendation of Sir John Lambert, in command of the troops with which he had been serving, and that he remained a lieutenant, serving on board the Forth frigate, with Sir William Bolton, Nelson's nephew. With Franklin's appointment in January 1818 to command the hired brig Trent, fitting out to accompany Captain Buchan in the Dorothea, Franklin's career as an Arctic explorer commenced. Their instructions were to pass between Spitzbergen and Greenland, use their best endeavours to reach the pole, and thence, if possible, to shape a course direct for Behring's Straits. The two ships sailed on 25 April, sighted Spitzbergen on 26 May, and passed without difficulty along its western coast; they were then stopped by the ice, and, being driven into the pack on 30 July, the Dorothea received so much damage as to be in momentary danger of foundering. They got into Dane's Gat, where such repairs as were possible were executed, but it was still very doubtful whether she could live through the passage home, and further contact with the ice was clearly out of the question. Buchan's instructions fully authorised him in this contingency to move into the Trent and send the Dorothea home; but he was unwilling to appear to desert his shipmates in a time of great danger. The Dorothea's state was such as to forbid her being sent home unattended, and Franklin's request that he might be allowed to go on rendered the task of superseding him the more disagreeable. So Buchan judged rightly that his proper course was to take the Dorothea home, with the Trent in close attendance on her. They arrived in England on 22 Oct.

Early in the following year Franklin was appointed to the command of an exploring expedition to be sent out with the general idea of amending the very defective geography of the northern part of America, and with more particular instructions 'to determine the latitudes and longitudes of the northern coast of North America, and the trendings of that coast from the mouth of the Coppermine River to the eastern extremity of that continent.' The details of the route from York Factory, named as a starting-point, were left to Franklin's judgment, guided by the advice he should receive from the agents of the Hudson's Bay Company, who would be instructed to co-operate with the expedition, and to provide it with guides, hunters, clothing, and ammunition. The small party, including Dr. (afterwards Sir John) Richardson, Hood and Back, midshipmen, the last of whom had been with Franklin in the Trent, two seamen, and four Orkney boatmen, landed at York on 30 Aug. 1819, and started on 9 Sept. The scheme was, with portable boats or canoes, to follow the line of rivers and lakes, beginning with the Nelson and Saskatchewan, and ending with the Elk, Slave, and Coppermine. At Cumberland House, a long-established station on the Saskatchewan, it was found that further progress that season was impossible. One of the seamen and the Orkneymen were sent back, and, leaving Hood and Richardson to bring on the boats when the way should be open, Franklin and Back started on foot for Fort Chipewyan on the shore of Lake Athabasca, which they reached on 26 March 1820. It was Franklin's intention to make all arrangements for an onward march as soon as the boats should arrive. He now found that owing to the rivalry, amounting almost to war, between the two trading companies which disputed the territory, no supplies were available; and, when the boats came on, the expedition left Fort Chipewyan on 18 July with little more than one day's provisions and with a scanty supply of powder. On 2 Aug. they left Fort Providence on the northern shore of Great Slave Lake, the party consisting, what with Canadian voyageurs and interpreters, of twenty-eight men, besides three women and three children. The next day they were joined by a large party of Indian hunters, under a chief Akaitcho. The progress was very slow, and the winter came on earlier than usual. By 25 Aug. the pools were beginning to freeze, and, though Franklin was anxious at all hazards to push on to the sea and establish himself for the winter at the mouth of the Coppermine, he yielded to the very urgent remonstrances of Akaitcho, and wintered in a hut which is still shown on the map as Fort Enterprise. It was not till 14 June 1821 that the ice gave way sufficiently for them to launch their canoes on the Coppermine, and to bid farewell to Akaitcho and his Indians. By 14 July they came within sight of the sea, and on the 21st embarked for their voyage in the Arctic Ocean. And so to the eastward in a tedious navigation along the coast, naming Cape Barrow and Cape Flinders, as far as Cape Turnagain, which they reached on 18 Aug.; when Franklin, finding that his resources would admit neither of going on nor of going back to the Coppermine, determined to take his way by a river to which he gave the name of his young companion, Hood. Hood's river was soon found to be impracticable for navigation. They took the large canoes to pieces, built two small ones which they could carry with them, reduced their baggage as much as possible, and began their march for Fort Providence through the country which has the distinction of being labelled, even in the Arctic, as 'Barren Grounds.' The story of their sufferings is one of the most terrible on human record. Cold, hunger, and fatigue broke down even the strongest of the party. Some died, some were murdered—poor Hood among the number, one was put to death as the murderer. In their last extremity Franklin and Richardson fell in with Akaitcho, who fed them, took care of them, and brought them in safety to Fort Providence on 11 Dec. Back and the miserable remnant of their party joined a few days later. They rested there for some months, and reached York again on 14 June 1822. 'Thus terminated,' wrote Franklin, 'our long, fatiguing, and disastrous travels in North America, having journeyed by water and land (including our navigation of the Polar Sea) 5,550 miles.'

In the following October Franklin, with his companions, arrived in England. He had already, during his absence (1 Jan. 1821), been made a commander; he was now (20 Nov.) advanced to post rank, in recognition of his labours and sufferings; he was also elected a fellow of the Royal Society. Richardson was appointed surgeon of the Chatham division of marines, and Back, who had been promoted to be a lieutenant, after three Arctic winters was sent out to the West Indies to be thawed. Franklin employed his time in England in writing the narrative of his journey, which was published early in the following year, and at once took its place among the most classic of books of travel. He also wooed and, in August 1823, was married to Miss Porden. Early in 1824 Franklin laid before the admiralty a scheme for another expedition, which might benefit by his previous experience, and possibly co-operate with the more purely naval expedition then fitting out under the command of Captain Parry. Franklin proposed that during the course of 1824 and the early months of 1825 stores, together with a party of English seamen, should be sent on in advance as far as possible; that he himself, starting in the spring, should go from New York to Lake Huron, and take on from the naval establishment there such further supplies as were available; and so, picking up his party as he proceeded, make his way to the Great Bear Lake, down the Mackenzie river, and along the coast westward as far as Kotzebue Sound, where a ship might be sent to meet him. In accordance with this the instructions were drawn out; the Blossom was commissioned for the service in Behring's Straits; and the previous arrangements having been made, Franklin, again with Back and Richardson, and with Mr. Kendall, a mate, as a third colleague, sailed from Liverpool on 16 Feb. 1825.

His wife, who had some months before given birth to a daughter, was now in an advanced decline; but he had probably persuaded himself that her illness was not necessarily mortal, and was much shocked by the news of her death, which reached him at the station on Lake Huron. He pushed on to join his advanced party with the boats, which he found near Fort Methy on 29 June. On 7 Aug. they reached Fort Norman on the Mackenzie, and leaving a party to build huts by Great Bear Lake, Franklin himself went down the river, a run of six days, to the sea; and landing on an island—which he named Garry Island, after the deputy-governor of the Hudson's Bay Company—he there planted the British flag, a silk union-jack which had been worked for the express purpose by his deceased wife. 'I will not,' he wrote, 'attempt to describe my emotions as it expanded to the breeze.' For the sake of his companions, however, he endeavoured to simulate cheerfulness; and after examining the archipelago at the mouth of the river, returned to the winter quarters, which he had intended naming Fort Reliance, but which, in his absence, the officers had named Fort Franklin.

The winter passed not unpleasantly; they had a sufficiency of clothing and food, and were able to keep open their communications with the posts of the Hudson's Bay Company, and to get occasional letters from home. As the summer approached, their preparations for the coming voyage were made, and they started on 24 June 1826, with the boats provisioned for eighty days at full allowance. At the head of the delta on 3 July they separated, Richardson and Kendall going eastwards as far as the Coppermine River and returning to Fort Franklin overland; while Franklin and Back went westwards, examining the coast as far as Point Beechey, in longitude 149° 37°'W. It was then 16 Aug.; there appeared no possibility of fetching Kotzebue Inlet; the hazard of shipwreck increased each day; wintering on the coast, as was suggested in their instructions, was out of the question; and a winter journey overland to Fort Franklin was an alternative which Franklin's past experience warned him against. One of the Blossom's boats had at this time advanced to the immediate neighbourhood of Point Barrow, but of this Franklin was of course ignorant; fortunately so, he thought afterwards; for otherwise he would have advanced, but would, in all probability, have been unable to overtake the Blossom's party. As it was, he returned to Fort Franklin by the way he had come. Richardson had been before him and had started again on a geologising expedition to Great Slave Lake. Franklin, remaining at the fort till 20 Feb. 1827, set out on foot for Fort Chipewyan, whence on 18 June he reached Cumberland House. There he rejoined Richardson, and the two, returning by way of Montreal and New York, where they were splendidly fêted, arrived in Liverpool on 26 Sept. The rest of the expedition, which had lost only two men, arrived at Portsmouth a fortnight later in charge of Captain Back. The journey, not so exciting nor so tragic as the former, had been even richer in geographical results, as was fully shown when the narrative was published in 1828. The Geographical Society of Paris awarded Franklin their gold medal; on 29 April 1829 he received the honour of knighthood; and at the summer convocation, the university of Oxford conferred on him the honorary degree of D.C.L. It was also during this period of relaxation that, on 5 Nov. 1828, he married Miss Griffin.

From August 1830 to December 1833 Franklin commanded the Rainbow frigate on the Mediterranean station, and during most of the time was employed on the coast of Greece, a service for which he received the order of the Redeemer of Greece, and afterwards (25 Jan. 1836) the Hanoverian Guelphic order. In the summer of 1836 he was appointed lieutenant-governor of Van Diemen's Land, and arrived at Hobart Town on 6 Jan. 1837. The period of his government, extending over nearly seven years, was marked by many measures for the social and moral improvement of the colony, then still, to a great extent, a convict station. The condition of the convicts more especially was a subject which much occupied his attention, and his endeavours for humanising them were strenuously aided by the exertions and the liberal expenditure of his wife. For the better class of colonists he established a scientific society which has developed into the present Royal Society of Hobart Town; and not only founded but largely endowed a college, for which, at his request, Dr. Arnold of Rugby selected a head-master. By the colonists, as a body, he was much beloved. At the close of his period of service he embarked at Hobart Town on 3 Nov. 1843, 'amidst,' he wrote, 'a burst of generous and enthusiastic feeling.' After visiting several places on the coast, he crossed over to Port Phillip, then a very recent settlement, from which he sailed 10 Jan. 1844, and arrived at Portsmouth in the following June.

Arctic exploration was exciting special interest. The Erebus and Terror had come home from a remarkable voyage to the Antarctic, so that suitable ships were at once available there was, too, a stagnation in the shipping interest, and seamen were everywhere clamouring for employment. Back and Dease and Simpson and Ross had traced the northern coast-line of America almost in its entirety; little remained to be done to solve the problem of the north-west passage. Few capable men any longer doubted its actual existence; though whether, under any circumstances, it could be available for navigation was still problematical. The admiralty resolved on a naval expedition. There was at first some hesitation about the commander; but Franklin claimed the post, as being the senior officer of Arctic experience then in England. The first lord of the admiralty pointed out to him that he was sixty years of age. 'No, no, my lord,' answered Franklin, 'only fifty-nine.' 'Before such earnestness all scruples yielded; the offer was officially made and accepted', and on 3 March 1845 Franklin commissioned the Erebus for 'particular service,' the Terror being at the same time commissioned by Captain Crozier.

The two ships, fitted, for the first time in the annals of Arctic exploration, with auxiliary screws, and provisioned (as it was believed) for three years, sailed together from Greenhithe on 18 May, with instructions to make their way to about 74°

N., 98° W., in the vicinity of Cape Walker, and thence to the southward and westward in a course as direct to Behring's Straits as ice and land might permit. 'It was well known,' wrote Sherard Osborn in 1859, 'that this southern course was that of Franklin's predilection, founded on his judgment and experience. There are many in England who can recollect him pointing on his chart to the western entrance of Simpson Strait and the adjoining coast of North America and saying, "If I can but get down there, my work is done; thence it's plain sailing to the westward."' In the beginning of July the ships were at Disco, and Fitzjames, the commander of the Erebus, wrote on the 12th 'that Sir John was delightful;' that both officers and men were in good spirits and of excellent material (Osborn, p. 286). On 26 July the ships parted from an Aberdeen whaler off the entrance of Lancaster Sound; a fair wind bore them away westward, and they vanished into the unknown. Over their movements a dark curtain settled down, which was raised slowly and with difficulty, nor was it fully lifted for fourteen years.

As early as the winter of 1846–7 there were gloomy anticipations; and though it was maintained at the admiralty that, as the ships were provisioned for three years, there were no grounds for anxiety, popular feeling so far prevailed that in the summer of 1847 large supplies, under the charge of Sir John Richardson and Dr. Rae, were sent out to Hudson's Bay to be conveyed by the inland water route to the mouth of the Mackenzie or of the Coppermine, or to other stations on the coast. As the winter of 1847–8 passed by without any news of the ships, a very real uneasiness was felt. With the spring of 1848 began a series of relief and search expeditions, both public and private, English and American, which has no parallel in maritime annals, and which, while prosecuting the main object of the voyages, turned the map of the Arctic regions north of America from a blank void into a grim but distinct representation of islands, straits, and seas. These expeditions, of which a complete list is given by Richardson (Polar Regions,

p. 172), may be summarised thus: One in 1847, that already mentioned from Hudson's Bay under Richardson and Rae; five in 1848; three in 1849; ten in 1850, including those sent out by the admiralty under Austin, Ommanney, Collinson, and McClure; two in 1851; nine in 1852, including the one under Sir Edward Belcher; five in 1853, including one in boats and sledges by Dr. Rae, and one into Smith's Sound by Dr. Kane of the United States Navy; two in 1854; one in 1855; and one, that of the Fox, in 1857.

In 1850 Captain Ommanney discovered on Beechey Island the traces of the missing ships having there passed their first winter, and at the same time vast stacks of preserved meat canisters, which, there was only too much reason to believe, had been found to be filled with putrid abomination, and had been there condemned by survey, thus fatally diminishing the three years' provisions which were supposed to be on board (ib. p. 163). Nothing further was learned till April 1854, when Dr. Rae, a factor of the Hudson's Bay Company, in a boat expedition carried on at the company's expense, gathered intelligence of a party of white men having been seen, four winters before, travelling over the ice near King William's Land, and of their bodies having been afterwards seen on the main land in the neighbourhood of a large river, presumably Back's Great Fish River. From the Eskimos who told him of this, Rae also obtained numerous small articles, silver spoons, &c., the marks on which clearly identified them as having belonged to officers of the Erebus and Terror; among others a small silver plate engraved 'Sir John Franklin, K.C.H.' (*Journal of the Royal Geographical Society*, 13 Nov. 1854, xxv. 250).

By these visible tokens the substantial truth of the story seemed to be fully confirmed, and the admiralty declined to enter on any further search. Others, however, were fain to hope that some survivors might still remain, and, chiefly by the personal exertions and at the personal cost of Lady Franklin, the Fox yacht was fitted out in 1857, under the command of

Captain (now Admiral Sir) Leopold McClintock. She failed through the accident of the seasons to get into the prescribed locality in the first or second year. It was not till the early months of 1859 that McClintock and his colleagues, Lieutenant Hobson of the navy, and Captain (now Sir) Allen Young of the mercantile marine, came on distinct traces of the lost expedition. Numerous relics were then found: a boat, a few skeletons, chronometers, clothing, instruments, watches, plate, books; and at last, towards the end of May, a written paper, the contents of which, together with what was told by the Eskimos or could be argued by induction, comprise the sum of all that can be known. The paper, which was one of the official forms issued to be left for transmission by any casual finder, had been in the first instance filled up in the customary manner, but carelessly and with a wrong date: '28 May 1847—H.M. ships Erebus and Terror wintered in the ice in lat. 70° 05o'N., long. 98° 23o W. Having wintered in 1846–7 [a mistake for 1845–6] at Beechey Island in lat. 74° 43o'28' N., long. 91° 39o'15' W., after having ascended Wellington Channel to lat. 77° and returned by the west side of Cornwallis Island. Sir John Franklin commanding the expedition. All well. . . .'

In 1846 they proceeded to the south-west, and eventually reached within twelve miles of the north extreme of King William's Land, when their progress was arrested by the approaching winter; and there they remained. The rest of the story was written on the margin of the same form by Captain Fitzjames: '25 April 1848—H.M. ships Terror and Erebus were deserted on 22 April, 5 leagues N.N.W. of this, having been beset since 12 Sept. 1846. The officers and crews, consisting of 105 souls, under the command of Captain F. R. M. Crozier, landed here in lat. 69° 37o 42" N., long. 98° 41o W. Sir John Franklin died on 11 June 1847, and the total loss by deaths in the expedition has been to this date 9 officers and 15 men.' To which was added, in Crozier's writing, 'and start on to-morrow, 26th, for Back's Fish River.' And this was all. From the Eskimos

McClintock learned that one of the ships sank in deep water, and that, to their grief, they got nothing from her; the other, much broken, was forced on shore, and from her they obtained the wood and iron which he saw in their possession. But there was no further news of the men. It was too certain that every soul of the party perished miserably; some earlier on King William's Land; some 'falling down and dying as they walked,' as an old woman told McClintock; many on the mainland by the Great Fish River. Most fortunate then in his end was Franklin, who died before this terrible fate fell on his men; died, proud in the consciousness of having seen, even if he had not fully travelled over the north-west passage, the strait separating King William's Land from Victoria Land; the strait which, if the ice would have permitted, would have led him into the known waters already explored by Dease and Simpson.

Since the finding of this written record Franklin has been recognised as the discoverer of the north-west passage, and is so styled on the pedestal of the statue to his memory erected at the public cost in Waterloo Place, London. This statue 'gives a tolerably faithful representation of him.' There are other statues at Hobart Town and Spilsby. A portrait painted by T. Phillips, R.A., about the time of his first marriage, has been photographed. Another portrait by John Jackson, R.A., lent by Mr. John Murray, was exhibited in the loan exhibition at South Kensington in 1868. Another portrait by Derby is engraved for Jerdan's 'National Portrait Gallery' (vol. ii.), and there is a capital lithograph by Negelen. A monument in Westminster Abbey, erected by his widow, was uncovered a fortnight after her death in 1875.

Franklin was a man not only of iron resolution and indomitable courage, but of a singular geniality, uprightness, and simplicity, which kindled into the warmest affection his influence over his comrades and subordinates. He left but one child, the daughter of his first wife. She married in 1849 the Rev. John Philip Gell, the head of an old Derbyshire family, who, as a young man, had been selected by Dr. Arnold's advice to be principal of the college in Hobart Town, and was long rector of Buxted in Sussex. Mrs. Gell died in 1860, leaving several children.

A biography from
Dictionary of National Biography, 1885-1900

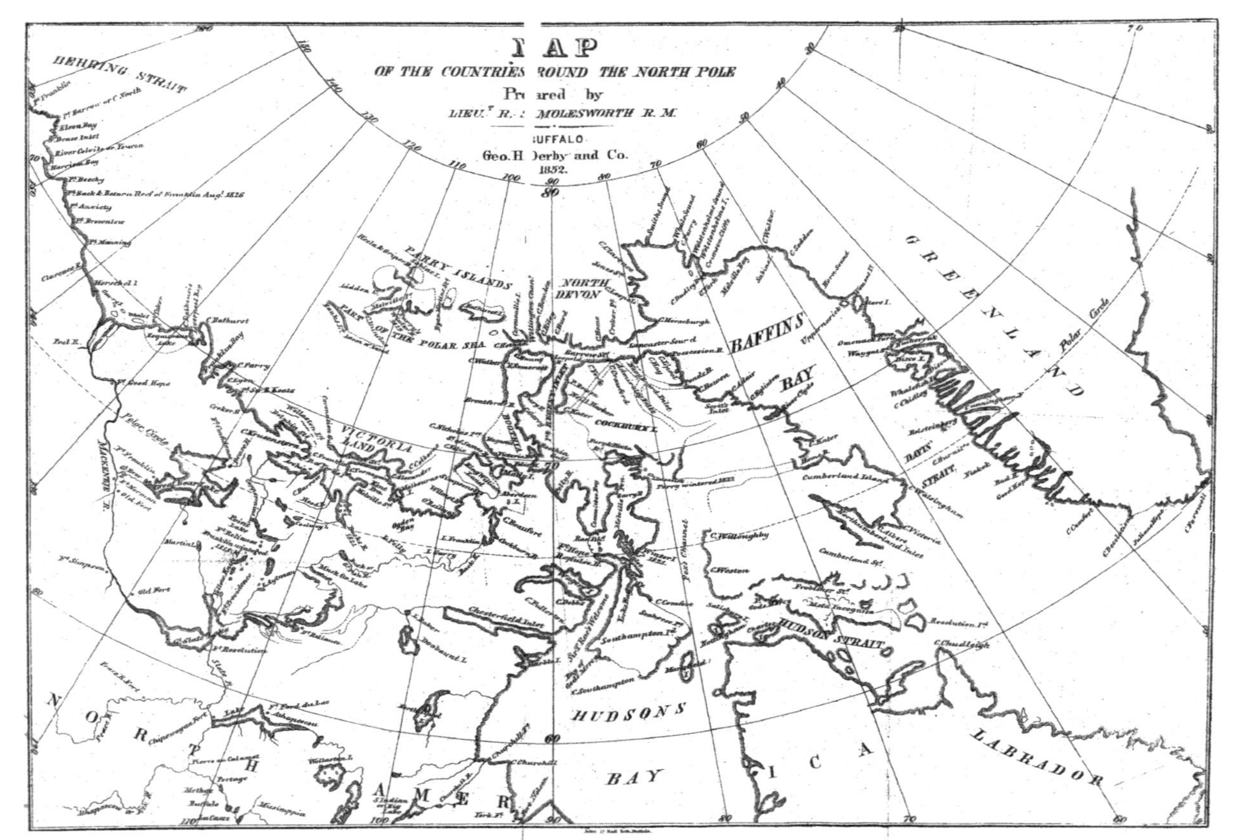
MAP
OF THE COUNTRIES ROUND THE NORTH POLE
Prepared by
LIEU.T R. MOLESWORTH R. M.
BUFFALO
Geo. H. Derby and Co.
1852.
BEHRING STRAIT
PARRY ISLANDS
NORTH DEVON
PART OF THE POLAR SEA
BAFFINS BAY
GREENLAND
DAVIS' STRAIT
VICTORIA LAND
BOOTHIA
COCKBURN I.
HUDSON STRAIT
HUDSONS BAY
LABRADOR
NORTH AMERICA
MACKENZIE R.
Polar Circle
Lancaster Sound
Cumberland Island
Chesterfield Inlet
Southampton I.
Melville Bay
Smith's Sound
Coronation Gulf
Fox's Channel

THE POLAR REGIONS

OR,
A SEARCH AFTER
SIR JOHN FRANKLIN'S EXPEDITION

DEDICATION.

ACCEPT, my dear Lady Franklin, these few pages, as the warm and honest tribute of deserved admiration for yourself and estimable niece, Miss Sophia Cracroft—admiration, which I delight in, in common with thousands, that such as you are Englishwomen; and pride, that a sailor's wife should so nobly have fulfilled her duty; for, if, on the one hand, the name of Sir John Franklin, that chief "*sans peur et sans reproche*," is dearly associated with our recollections of the honours won in the ice-bound regions of the Pole, your names are not the less so, with the noble efforts made to rescue, or solve the fate of our missing countrymen.

That those sacrifices, those untiring exertions, that zeal which has never wavered, that hope so steadfast, since it is that of an Englishwoman for her husband, that patience under misconstruction, that forgiveness for the sneer of jealousy, and that pity for the malicious, which you have so pre-eminently displayed, may yet, by God's help, one day reap its reward in the accomplishment of your wishes, is the fervent prayer of

SHERARD OSBORN.

PREFACE.

I FEAR with the many of my cloth, my crime in writing a book will be an unpardonable one; the more so, that I cannot conscientiously declare, that it has been at the urgent desire of my friends, &c., that I have thus made my début.

My motive is twofold: to tell of the doings of a screw steam-vessel, the first ever tried in the Polar regions, and by a light, readable description of incidents in the late search for Sir John Franklin, to interest the general reader and the community at large upon that subject. Without fear, favour, or affection, I have told facts as they have occurred; and I trust have, in doing so, injured no man. A journal must necessarily be, for the most, a dry narration of facts; I have, therefore, thrown in here and there general observations and remarks founded upon such facts, rather than a dry repetition of them.

To the officers and men serving under my command, I can offer no higher compliment than in having thus placed their severe and zealous labours before the public; and no professional reader who reads these "Stray Leaves," can fail, I am certain, to perceive how heavily must have fallen the labours here recounted upon the men and officers of the steam tenders, and how deep an obligation I their commander must be under to them for their untiring exertions, by which this, the first and severe trial of steam in the Arctic règions, was brought to a successful issue.

The "Resolutes," no doubt, will object to the round terms in which I have growled at the bluff-bowed vessel it was my fate and now my pride to have towed so many miles in the Frozen Zone; but on second thoughts, I doubt not they will acquit me, for they will remember the joke was once on their side; and if I do not love their *ship*, at any rate I liked *them*.

To Lieutenant W. May and Mr. M'Dougal, I am much indebted for their faithful sketches. I fear my letter-press is unworthy of the companionship.

To those who may accuse me of egotism in confining my remarks so much to the achievements of my own vessel, I have merely to say, that in doing so, I was best able to be truthful; but that I am fully aware that to the other screw steamer, the "Intrepid," and my gallant friend and colleague, Commander J. B. Cator, there fell an equal amount of labour; and that to all, ships as well as screws, there was an equal proportion of hardship, danger, and privation. I should indeed be forgetful as well as ungrateful, did I here fail to acknowledge the more than kindness and assistance I have ever experienced from my friend Mr. Barrow, a name past and present inseparably connected with our Arctic discoveries; so likewise I have to offer my thanks, heartfelt as they are sincere, to those who, like Admiral Sir Francis Beaufort and Captain Hamilton of the Admiralty, bade me speed, when sincerity and zeal was all I had to boast, and who dared to overlook the crime of youth, and granted to "seven-and-twenty" the deference which "five-and-fifty" alone can claim.

RICHMOND, *Feb.* 15, 1852.

STRAY LEAVES

FROM

AN ARCTIC JOURNAL.

THE evils attendant on a hurried outfit and departure, as is the usual man-of-war custom, were in no wise mitigated in the case of the Royal Naval Expedition, fitted out at Woolwich, in 1850, to search for Sir John Franklin's Squadron; and a general feeling of joy at our departure prevailed amongst us, when, one fine morning, we broke ground from Greenhithe.

The "Resolute" and "Assistance" had a couple of steamers to attend upon them; whilst we, the "Pioneer" and "Intrepid," screwed and sailed, as requisite to keep company. By dark of the 4th of May, 1850, we all reached an anchorage near Yarmouth; and the first stage of our outward journey was over.

No better proof of the good feeling which animated our crews can be adduced than the unusual fact of not a man being missing amongst those who had originally entered,—not a desertion had taken place,—not a soul had attempted to quit the vessels, after six months' advance had been paid.

Here and there amongst the seamen a half-sleepy indifference to their work was observable. This I imputed to the reaction after highly sentimental "farewells," in which, like other excesses, Jack delights; the women having, as usual, done all they could, by crying alongside, to make the men believe they were running greater risks than had ever been before undergone by Arctic navigators.

The old seamen's ditty of—

"We sailed by Fairlĕe, by Beachĕy, and Dungĕness,
Until the North Foreland light we did see"—

gives a very good idea of our progress from beacon to lighthouse, and lighthouse to headland, until the lofty coast of Yorkshire sunk under the lee; and by the 8th of May the squadron was making slow progress across the mouth of the Frith of Forth. Hitherto, "all had been pleasant as a marriage bell;" the weather had been fine; and we already calculated our days of arrival at different points, as if the calm was to last for ever. The Cheviot Hills glittered in the west; it was the kind good-bye of our own dear England. Hundreds of white sails dotted a summer sea: all was joyous and sparkling. Scotland greeted us with a rough "nor'-wester,"—and away we went. "Not all the king's horses" could have kept the expedition together.

The "Resolute" and "Assistance," hauled dead on a wind, under close-reefed topsails, performed a stationary movement, called "pile-driving" by sailors, which, as the pilot suggested, would, if the breeze lasted, carry them to the coast of Holland. The two steam vessels, under fore-and-aft canvas, drew away rapidly to windward and ahead, and in spite of all we could do, a few hours of darkness effectually succeeded in dispersing us. Accident again brought the "Pioneer" in sight of the vessels for a few hours; but the "Intrepid" found herself in Stromness Harbour, with a degree of celerity which gave rise to a racing disposition on the part of my gallant colleague, "Intrepid," *versus* "Pioneer," which it took a great many days of competition to decide.

They who want excitement had better go and beat a vessel up the Pentland Firth, against both wind and tide. I tried it, but shall not repeat the experiment; and, after a thorough good shaking in the North Sea, was not sorry to find myself at anchor in Stromness.

The very proper and triste Sabbath of the North was followed by a busy Monday. The arrival of so many gold cap-bands, and profusion of gilt buttons, interfered, I fear materially, with the proper delivery of the morning milk and butter by sundry maidens with golden locks; and the purser's wholesale order for beef threatened to create a famine in the Orkneys. The cheapness of whiskey appeared likely to be the cause of our going to sea with a crew in a lamentable state of drunkenness, and rather prejudiced me against Stromness; but if it had no other redeeming quality, all its faults would be forgotten in the astounding fact that *there* may be found a landlady with moderate prices and really fresh eggs.

As a description of this part of the world is no part of my task, I will pass over our long and crooked walk about Stromness; and the failure of the good folk there to induce us to trust ourselves on their ponies for a ride to Kirkwall, naturally limited our knowledge of the neighbourhood.

Above the town of Stromness rises a conical-shaped hill; it has, I believe, been immortalized by Scott in his "Pirate:" it had yet deeper interest for me, for I was told that up it had toiled dear friends now missing with Franklin. I and a kind shipmate walked out one evening to make our pilgrimage to a spot hallowed by the visit of the gallant and true-hearted that had gone before us—and, as amid wind and drizzle we scrambled up the hill, I pictured to myself how, five short years before, those we were now in search of had done the same. Good and gallant Gore! chivalrous Fitz-James! enterprising Fairholme! lion-hearted Hodgson! dear De Vaux! —Oh! that ye knew help was nigh!

We surmounted the hill—the Atlantic was before us, fierce and troubled; afar to seaward the breakers broke and lashed themselves against the firm foundation of the old Head of Hay, which loomed through mist and squall, whilst overhead the scream of sea-fowl, flying for shelter, told that the west wind would hold wild revelry that night.

"H. M. S. North Star," carved on the turf, showed where some of her people had chosen this spot for a record of their visit to Orkney; we did likewise, in honour of our own bonnie craft; and then, strolling homeward, discussed the probable chances of the existence of the said "North Star;" the conclusion arrived at being that there was more cause for anxiety on her account than for Franklin's Expedition, she having gone out totally unprepared for wintering, and with strict injunctions not to be detained: "l'homme propose, et Dieu dispose."

I could have hugged the snuffy old postmaster for a packet of letters he gave me. I rushed on board to a cabin which proved, as the First Lord had sagaciously remarked, into how small a space a Lieutenant Commanding could be packed; and, in spite of an unpaid tailor's bill, revelled in sweet and pleasant dreams.

The "Intrepid" and "Pioneer" rejoined the ships at Long-Hope; and my gallant comrade and I made a neck-and-neck race of it, showing that in steaming, at any rate, there would be little to choose between us; and, on May 15th, the Arctic squadron weighed, and, passing out of the Pentland Firth, the

"Dasher" and "Lightning" cheered us, took our letters,—and the Searching Expedition was alone steering for Greenland. Night threw her mantle around us; the lonely light of Cape Wrath alone indicating where lay our homes. I like losing sight of Old England by night. It is pleasant to go to rest with a sweet recollection of some quiet scene you have just dwelt upon with delight, the spirit yearning for the excitement and novelty ahead. You rise in the morning, old Ocean is around you: there is, to the seamen, a lullaby, say what they may, in his hoarse song; and they of the middle watch tell how the friendly light of some distant cape glimmered and danced in the east, until lost in some passing squall.

Now for the Northwest! we exclaimed,—its much talked of dangers,—its chapter of horrors! As gallant Frobisher says, "it is *still* the only thing left undone, whereby a notable mind might be made famous and remarkable." As it was in Frobisher's day, so it is now, unless Franklin has accomplished it, and lies beset off Cape Jakan—and why may it not be so?

Whilst the squadron progresses slowly towards Cape Farewell, the ships under topsails, and the steamers under jury-masts and sails, we will take a retrospective view of what is now—1850—going to be done for the relief of Franklin.

Capt. Collinson, with two ships, has gone to Behring's Straits with the "Plover" as a dépôt, in Kotzebue Sound, to fall back upon in case of disaster. He steers direct for Melville Island, along the coast of North America. Capt. Pullen, having successfully searched the coast from Point Barrow to the Mackenzie River, is endeavouring now to push from thence, in a northerly direction, for Bank's Land. Dr. Rae is to do the same from the Coppermine River. Capt.

Penny, a first-rate whaling captain, with two fast brigs, is now ahead of us, hoping to make an early passage across the middle ice of Baffin's Bay. He goes to Jones's Sound and Wellington Channel, to reach the Parry Isles by a northern route.

We go with two sailing ships and two steam vessels, so as to form separate divisions of two vessels each, to examine Barrow's Straits south-westerly to Cape Walker, westerly towards Melville Island, and north-westerly up Wellington Channel. Thus no less than eight fine ships flying the pendant, and two land parties are directed, by different routes, on Melville Island. Besides these, an American expedition, fitted out by that prince of merchants, Mr. Grinnell, leaves shortly for the same destination; and in Lady Franklin's own vessel, the "Prince Albert," as well as a craft under Sir John Ross, we find two more assistants in the plan of search.

And yet, gentle reader, if you turn to the papers of the fall of 1849, you will find some asserting that Sir John Franklin had perished in Baffin's Bay, because Sir James Ross had found nothing of him in Lancaster Sound! Happily the majority of Englishmen have, however, decided otherwise; and behold, this noble equipment! this magnificent outlay of men and material!

We will not dwell on the pleasures or annoyances of the cruise across the Atlantic, beyond stating the fact that our bluff-bowed worse-halfs, the sailing ships, nigh broke our hearts, as well as our hawsers, in dragging their breakwater frames along in the calms; and that we of the screws found our steam vessels all we could wish, somewhat o'er lively, mayhap,—a frisky tendency to break every breakable article on board. But there was a saucy swagger in them, as they bowled along the hollow of a western sea, which showed they had good blood in them; and we soon felt confident of disappointing those Polar seers, who had foretold shipwreck and disaster as their fate.

The appearance of numerous sea-birds,—the Tern especially, which do not fly far from land,—warned us, on Sunday 26th May, of our fast approach to Greenland, and on the morrow we espied the picturesque shores about Cape Farewell. Which of all the numerous headlands we saw was the identical cape, I do not pretend to say; but we chose, as *our* Cape Farewell, a remarkable-looking peak, with a mass of rock perched like a pillar upon its crest. The temperature began to fall as we advanced, and warmer coats quickly replaced our English clothing.

Distant as we were from Greenland, our view of its southern extremity was fleeting, but sufficient to show that it fully realized in appearance the most striking accumulation of ice and land that the mind could picture,—a land of gaunt famine and misery; but which nevertheless, for some good purpose, it had pleased Providence in a measure to people.

Had we not had an urgent duty to perform, I should have regretted thus hurrying past the land; for there is much to see there. True, Greenland has no deep historical interest, but the North has always had its charm for me. Scandinavia, and her deeds,—the skill and intrepidity of her bold Vikings,—their colonies in Snæland, our Iceland,—their discovery of Greenland,—and the legend of the pirate Biarni, who forestalled even the great Columbus in his discovery,—were all associated with the region through which we were now sailing.

Without compass, without chart, full three centuries before the Genoese crossed the Atlantic, the Norsemen, in frail and open barks, braved the dark and angry sea (which was so sorely tossing even our proud vessels); and, unchecked by tempest, by ice, or hardship, penetrated probably as far as we could in the present day. This, and much more, throws a halo of ancient renown around this lonely land; moreover, I had long loved Nature's handiworks, and here assuredly her wonders reward the traveller. Here, methought me of the mighty glacier, creeping on like Time, silently, yet ceaselessly; the deep and picturesque fiord pent up between precipices, huge, bleak, and barren; the iceberg! alone a miracle; then the great central desert of black lava and glittering ice, gloomy and unknown but to the fleet rein-deer, who seeks for shelter in a region at whose horrors the hardy natives tremble; and last, but not least, the ruins of the Scandinavian inhabitants, and the present fast disappearing race of "the Innuit," or Esquimaux. Dullard must he be who sees not abundance here to interest him.

Flirting with the first ice we saw, it soon appeared that the training of the uninitiated, like puppies, was to be a very formal and lengthy piece of business. Thanks to an immense deal of water, and very little ice, the steamers eventually towed the "Resolute" and the transport (a lively specimen of the genus), into the Whale-Fish Islands,—a group of rocky islets, some twenty miles distant from the excellent Danish harbour of Godhaab on the Island of Disco.

We did as our forefathers in anchoring at the Whale Fish Islands, but would strongly recommend those who visit this neighborhood to go to Godhaab rather. Its anchorage is good, communication with Europe a certainty, and the hospitality of the Danish residents, few though they be, cheering and pleasant to ship-sick wanderers.

Having thus expressed my total dissent from those who, with steam vessels, go to Whale-Fish Isles, it will be but fair for me to stay, that I arrived at this our first stage in the journey to the Nor'-West, in far from good humour. We had been twenty-four days from Greenhithe to Cape Farewell, and sixteen days from the latter point to our anchorage; hurry being out of the question when a *thing* like the "Emma Eugenia" was pounding the water in a trial of speed with perfect snuff-boxes, like the "Resolute" and "Assistance." Patience and a four-day tow had at last finished the work: and to all our anxious inquiries about the prospect of the season, as to where Penny was, and whether any intelligence had reached the settlements? not an answer was to be obtained from a besotted Danish carpenter, whose knowledge appeared to be limited to a keen idea of changing, under a system he called "Trock," sundries (with which the Danske Kœing had intrusted him) into blubber and seal-oil.

After a day of coal-dust, I landed with some others to see what was to be seen, and to load, as we were taught to believe, a boat with wild fowl. The principal settlement having been pointed out, we landed on the slope of one of the islands, on which a coarse rank vegetation existed amongst the numerous relics of departed seals, sacrificed to the appetites of the Esquimaux and the *trocking* of the Governor, as he was facetiously styled. The said individual soon appeared, and in spite of copious libations of Her Britannic Majesty's "Pure Jamaica," of which he had partaken, was most polite and hospitable. From him I discovered that he and a cooper were the only Danes residing here; and they, together with a cross-breed who did the double duty of priest and schoolmaster, constituted the officials of Cron-Prin's Islands. The native population amounted perhaps to one hundred souls: and it was in supplying their wants, and in affording a market for their superfluous skins and blubber, that the Danes derived a profit, under a strict system of monopoly; no foreigners being allowed to trade with the Esquimaux, and they, on the other hand, having strict injunctions to lodge every thing they do not require for private use, in the public store. The quantity of seal-blubber in store, which was equal to as much oil, amounted to nigh upon 100 tons; the number of seals annually destroyed must be enormous: this says much for the industry of the natives.

The Esquimaux appeared all comfortable and well to do, well clad, cleanly, and fat. Most of them had moved for a while into their summer lodges, which consist of little else than a seal-skin tent, clumsily supported with sticks. They were more than sufficiently warm; and the number of souls inhabiting one of these lodges appeared only to be limited by the circle of friends and connections forming a family. The winter abode—formed almost underground—appeared decidedly well adapted to afford warmth, and some degree of pure ventilation, in so severe a climate, where fuel can be spared only for culinary purposes; and I was glad to see that, although necessity obliges the Esquimaux to eat of the oil and flesh of the seal and naorwhal, yet, when they could procure it, they seemed fully alive to the gastronomic pleasures of a good wholesome meal off fish, birds' eggs, bread, sugar, tea, and coffee.

Their canoes are perfect models of beauty and lightness; in no part of the world do we see them excelled in speed and portability—two very important qualities in the craft of a savage; and in ornamental workmanship, the skill of both men and women is tastefully displayed.

The clothing of the natives is vastly superior to any thing we could produce, both in lightness of material, and wind and water-tight qualities;—the material, seal and deer skin, and entrails, manufactured by the women; their needles of Danish manufacture; their thread, the delicate sinews of animals. We gladly purchased all we could obtain of their clothing.

Every one has heard of the horrors of an Esquimaux existence,—sucking blubber instead of roast beef, train-oil heir usual beverage, and a seal their bonne-bouche; the long gloomy winter spent in pestiferous hovels, lighted and warmed with whale-oil lamps; the narrow gallery for an entrance, along which the occupant creeps for ingress and egress. This and much more has been told us; yet, now that I have seen it all,—the Esquimaux's home, the Esquimaux's mode of living, and the Esquimaux himself,—I see nothing so horrible in one or the other.

The whaler, from bonnie Scotia, or busy Hull, fresh from the recollection of his land and home, no doubt shudders at the comparative misery and barbarity of these poor people; but those who have seen the degraded Bushmen or Hottentots of South Africa, the miserable Patanies of Malayia, the Fuegians or Australians of our southern hemisphere, and remember the comparative blessings afforded by nature to those melancholy specimens of the human family, will, I think, exclaim with me, that the Esquimaux of Greenland are as superior to them in mental capacity, manual dexterity, physical enterprise, and social virtues, as the Englishman is to the Esquimaux.

The strongest—indeed, I am assured, the only—symptom of the advantage of religious instruction perceptible in the Greenlander, over his North American brethren, is in the respect they show for the marriage tie, and strong affection for their children. The missionary, with this race, appears to have few difficulties to contend with: naturally gentle, and without any strong superstitious prejudices, they receive without resistance the simple creed of Reformed religion, which he has spread amongst them; and the poor Esquimaux child sends up its prayers and thanksgiving, in the words taught us by our Saviour, as earnestly and confidently as the educated offspring of Englishmen.

An old man, whom I pressed to accompany me as pilot to the Island of Disco, declined, under the plea that his wife was very ill, and that there was no one but himself to take care of the "piccaninny." Interested from such proper feeling in the man, Dr. P—— and I entered his winter abode, which he apologized for taking us to,—the illness of his "cara sposa" having prevented him changing his residence for the usual summer tent. Crawling on all fours through a narrow passage, on either side of which a dog-kennel and a cook-house had been constructed, we found ourselves in an apartment, the highest side of which faced us, the roof gradually sloping down to the ground.

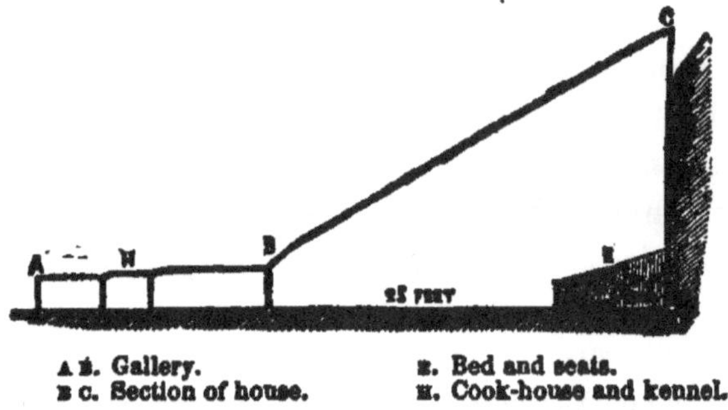

A B. Gallery. E. Bed and seats.
B C. Section of house. H. Cook-house and kennel.

The above section will give some idea of the place. Along one side of the abode a sort of bed-place extended for its whole length, forming evidently the family couch; for on one end of it, with her head close to a large seal-oil lamp, was the sick woman. She was at the usual Esquimaux female's employment of feeding the flame with a little stick from a supply of oil, which would not rise of its own accord up the coarse and ill-constructed wick; over the flame was a compound, which the sufferer told us was medicine for her complaint,—the rheumatism, a very prevalent one amongst these people. Leaving the kind Doctor to do the part of a good Samaritan, I amused myself with looking over the strange home into which I had got. The man took much pride in showing me his family,—consisting of a girl and three fine boys. His wife, he assured me, was only twenty-eight years of age: she looked at least six-and-thirty; and he likewise, though only thirty-four, had the appearance of being at least ten years older. They had married when she was twenty,—the usual age for marriage, as he told me. His daughter, rather a pretty and slight-made girl, was very busy making shoes for her brothers out of cured skin. I rewarded the youthful sempstress by giving her one of a number of dolls kindly sent me for the purpose by Mrs. W. of Woolwich; and could that kind friend have seen the joyful countenance of the Esquimaux child, she would indeed have been richly remunerated for her thoughtful little addition to my stock of presents. To finish my Esquimaux tale, I was next day not a little surprised at the father coming on board, and giving me a small pouch which his child had sewn for me in return for my present. This proved at least that Esquimaux children can appreciate kindness as well as others.

The Whale-Fish group consist of a congery of islets, of various shapes and sizes, with deep water channels between; the whole of granitic formation, with broad veins of quartz and masses of gneiss overlaying in various directions. Those I visited exhibited proof of constant and, I might say, rapid destruction from the action of water and frost. The southern and south-west sides of the larger islands were of, may be, 300 or 400 feet elevation, with a gradual dip to the north-east, as if their creation had been brought about by some submarine agency upheaving the primary rock, with an irregular force from the north-east.

The tallest cliffs were rent from crown to base, and frost-cracks intersected one another in such a perfect labyrinth, that the whole mass appeared as if merely hanging together from its stupendous weight. The narrow bays and bights with a southern aspect, where the concussion of a heavy sea had had its effect, were strewn with the wreck of the adjacent precipices, and progress for sportsmen along the shore, in pursuit of wild fowl, was extremely difficult. On the northern sides, these islands showed other features quite as peculiar to the glacial region upon which we were wandering: there the low projecting ledges of granite were polished by the constant attrition of oceanic ice and icebergs, until walking over them became barely possible.

June 18*th*, 1850.—I am much amused at the ease with which we assimilate ourselves to new climates and new habits. Yesterday, my friend Dr. P—— and I bathed within fifty yards of an iceberg, the water only two degrees above freezing point; candour must acknowledge that we did not stay long; and to-night, though no Highlander in love of hardship, I found myself at midnight in the water groping for lost gun-gear, an experiment which, having escaped from without rheumatism, I promise not to repeat. One of my crew slept last night on deck with his arm for a pillow, although the temperature was below freezing point, and every one complains of heat and throws aside jacket and cap when making the slightest exertion.

Coal-dust every where and on every thing. Incessant work from 4, A. M., to 8 or 9 o'clock, P. M., one would have supposed, would have induced rational beings to go quietly to bed when the day's work was over. It was far otherwise.

The novelty of constant daylight, and the effect which it always has upon the system, until accustomed to it, of depriving one of the inclination to go to roost at regular hours, told upon us, and often have I found myself returning from five hours' work, chasing, shooting, and pulling a boat, just as the boatswain's mates were piping "stow hammocks!" That I was not singular, a constant discharge of guns throughout the night well proved, and unhappy nights must the ducks and dovekies have spent during our stay.

Not to shoot became, in the Arctic squadron, tantamount to folly, although the proceeds of great consumption of powder were but small; nevertheless, stout men, who had not buttoned a gaiter since their youth, were to be seen rivalling chamois-hunters in the activity with which they stalked down the lady ducks on their nests. Apoplexy was forgotten, the tender wife's last injunction on the subject of dry feet pitched to the winds, and rash men of five-and-forty pulled and shot little birds, in leaky punts, with all the energy of boys of fifteen.

Cold fingers, and a load of Flushing cloth on one's back, are vile realities; otherwise I could have given fancy her swing, and spent many an hour in the "blest ideal," at the beautiful and novel scene which lay around me on a lovely morning at one o'clock. I had just crossed to the north side of an island which faces Greenland, and passed a quiet and secluded bay, at whose head the remains of a deserted ruin told of the by-gone location of some Esquimaux fishermen, whose present home was shown by here and there a grave carefully piled over with stones to ward off dog and bear. All was silent, except the plaintive mew of the Arctic sea-swallow as it wheeled over my head, or the gentle echo made by mother ocean as she rippled under some projecting ledge of ice. The snow, as it melted amongst the rocks behind, stole quietly on to the sea through a mass of dark-coloured moss; whilst a scanty distribution of pale or delicately-tinted flowers showed the humble flora of the north. The sun, sweeping along the heavens opposite, at a very low altitude, gilded as it rose the snowy crests of the mountains of Disco, and served to show, more grim and picturesque, the naturally dark face of the "Black Land of Lively." From thence round to the east, in the far horizon, swept the shores of Greenland, its glaciers, peaks, and headlands, all tortured by mirage into a thousand fantastic shapes, as if Dame Nature had risen from her couch in frolicsome mood. Between this scene and my feet, icebergs of every size and shape, rich with fretting of silvery icicle, and showing the deepest azure tint or richest emerald, strewed a mirror-like sea, glowing with the pale pink of morning.

The awful silence was impressive: unwilling to break it I sat me down.

> "I felt her presence by its spell of might,
> Stoop o'er me from above—
> The calm majestic presence of the night,
> As of the one I love."

Suddenly a distant roar boomed along the water and echoed amongst the rocks: again and again I heard it, when, to my astonishment, several huge icebergs in the offing commenced to break up. A fearful plunge of some large mass would clothe the spot in spray and foam; a dull reverberating echo pealed on; and then, merely from the concussion of the still air, piece after piece detached itself from icebergs far and near, and the work of demolition was most rapid: truly did Baffin boast, that he had laid open one of Nature's most wonderful laboratories; and I thought with Longfellow, in his Hyperion,—

"The vast cathedral of nature is full of holy scriptures and shapes of deep mysterious meaning: all is solitary and silent there. Into this vast cathedral comes the human soul seeking its Creator, and the universal silence is changed to sound, and the sound is harmonious and has a meaning, and is comprehended and felt."

After many difficulties, which called for some obstinacy on my part to master, I was allowed to go to Disco, and Captain Ommaney, hearing of my intention, kindly made up a party. Taking one of our boats, we shipped an Esquimaux pilot, called "Frederick," and started on June 21st, at 2 o'clock in the morning. To all our inquiries about Disco, Frederick had but one reply,—"by and by you see." He liked rum and biscuit, and was only to be animated by the conversation turning upon seals, or *poussies*, as the natives call them. Then indeed Frederick's face was wreathed in smiles, or rather its oleaginous coat of dirt cracked in divers directions, his tiny eyes twinkled, and he descanted, in his broken jargon, upon the delight of *poussey* with far more unction than an alderman would upon turtle. After threading the islets we struck to north-east by compass, from the northernmost rock of the group, which our guide assured us would sink below the horizon the moment of our arrival off Godhaab. He was perfectly right, for after four hours' pulling and sailing we found ourselves under a small look-out house, and the islets of our departure had dipped.

Entering a long and secure harbour, we reached a perfectly landlocked basin: in it rode a couple of Danish brigs, just arrived from Copenhagen, with stores for the settlement; and on the shores of this basin, the Danish settlement of Godhaab was situated, a few stores, and the residence of two or three officials,—gentlemen who superintended the commercial monopoly to which I have before referred: a flag-staff and some half-dozen guns formed the sum total.

Landing at a narrow wooden quay, close to which natives and sailors were busy unladening boats, we found ourselves amongst a rambling collection of wooden houses, built in Dano-Esquimaux style, with some twenty native lodges intermixed. Very few persons were to be seen moving about: we heard afterwards that the body of natives were seal-catching to the northward. A troop of half-caste boys and girls served, however, to represent the population, and in them the odd mixture of the Mongolian with the Scandinavian race was advantageously seen.

A Danish seaman conducted Captain O——, Dr. D——, and self, to the residence of the chief official, and, at the early hour of six, we made a formal visit.

His mansion was of wood, painted black, with a red border to the windows and roof: no doubt, so decorated for a good purpose; but the effect was more striking than pleasing. A low porch with double doors, two sharp turns in a narrow dark passage,—to baffle draughts, no doubt,—and we found ourselves in a comfortable room with Herr Agar smoking a cigar, and gaily attired to receive us. The "Herr" spoke but little English; we no Danish: however, the quiet and reserved manner of the good northern did not conceal a certain kindness of which he soon gave us hospitable proof; for, on acceding to his offer of a little coffee, we were surprised to see a nice tidy lady—his wife, as he informed us—spread a breakfast fit for a Viking, and then with gentle grace she ably did the honours of her board. Hang me, when I looked at the snow-white linen, the home-made cleanly cheer, the sweet wife all kindness and anxiety, I half envied the worthy Dane the peace and contentment of his secluded lot, and it needed not a glass of excellent Copenhagen schiedam to throw a "couleur de rose" about this Ultima Thule of dear woman's dominion.

The morning pull had given a keenness to our appetites, and I have a general recollection of rye bread, Danish cake, excellent Zetland butter, Dutch cheese, luscious ham, boiled potatoes, and Greenland trout fresh from the stream. Could sailors ask for or need more? I can only say that we all felt that, if Herr Agar and Madame Agar (I hate that horrid word Frau) would only borrow our last shilling, we were ready to lend it.

A broken conversation ensued, a little English and much Danish, when Dr. D—— fortunately produced Captain Washington's Esquimaux vocabulary, and, aided by the little son of our host, we soon twisted out all the news Herr Agar had to give.

Captain Penny had only stayed a short time. He arrived on May the 4th. The prospect of an early season was most cheering, and then the worthy Herr produced a piece of paper directed to myself by my gallant friend Penny. He wrote in haste to say his squadron had arrived, all well, after a splendid run from Aberdeen: he was again off, and sent kind remembrances, dated May 4th.

This, at any rate, was joyful intelligence, and worth my journey to Disco; my heart leaped with joy, and I thought, at any rate, if we were late, he was full early.

After a long chat, we went for a stroll, in which a tree—yes! as I live, a tree—was discovered. Be not envious, ye men of Orkney, it stood full thirteen inches high, and was indigenous, being the dwarf birch-tree, the monarch of an arctic forest! Stumbling upon the churchyard I should have indulged my taste for old tombstones, had not the musquitoes forbidden it; and, with a hurried glance at the names of old hunters of fish and departed Danes and Dutchmen, I ran for the beach, remarking that, whereas we in Europe evince respect for those who have preceded us to that bourne—

> "Where life's long journey turns to sleep,
> Nor weary pilgrim wakes to weep—"

by placing stones around their last homes, in Greenland pieces of soft and ugly wood are substituted, although nature has strewn on every side masses of granite fit to form mausoleums for Pharaohs. Bad taste! I exclaimed; but that's not confined to Disco.

Having promised to return to say good-bye, we kept our word most willingly, and found "Herr Agar" had a circle of friends to meet us; and my astonishment was great at the sight of *two more petticoats.* One was the wife of a Moravian missionary, and the other the wife of a gentleman at Jacob's Sound. They looked perfectly happy, and at least appeared as well at home in the dreary region which had become their adopted country, as we could expect, or their husbands desire. Conversation soon flagged; the missionary gave it up in despair; the "Herr" smoked in silence; and but for the ladies we should have been soon dumb. Happily for me (for I wanted to purchase some seal-skins), a captain of one of the brigs came in at the moment, and, understanding both English and Danish, conversation became quite animated. Watching my opportunity, I told him of my desire to purchase seal-skins for trowsers for my men; he immediately informed Herr Agar, who gave him a yah! and walked me off by the arm to his storerooms, followed by his good lady; lifting a bundle of beautiful seal-skins, the Herr made me an offer of them. I commenced fumbling for my purse, and at last produced some gold, making signs that various officers intended to have seal-skin trowsers. Nay! nay! exclaimed the good lady, thrusting back my money, whilst the Herr began loading me with skins. Oh! the horror of that moment: I felt as if I had been begging, and must have looked very like it, for Mrs. Agar, with a look of sudden inspiration, as if she perfectly understood me, ran off to her husband's wardrobe, and produced a pair of trowsers, of perfect Dutch dimensions, and, with the most innocent smile, made signs of how I should pull them on. I smiled, for they would have made a suit of clothes for me.

Seeing no way of getting out of the scrape my ignorance of Danish and their generosity had led me into, I determined to take as little as possible, and with a thousand thanks walked back to the drawing-room, with Herr Agar's "whisperables" on one arm and a couple of seal-skins on the other, my face burning, and my conscience smiting.

Time pressed, and we bid our kind friends good-bye. Herr Agar fired a salute of three guns, which we returned with three cheers; and, after taking a stirrup cup on board the "Peru," started for Whale-Fish Islands, which we reached at eleven o'clock at night, much pleased with our excursion.

Every one likes a souvenir of some pleasant by-gone scene or event: these souvenirs are often odd ones. A messmate of mine used to tell of Greece, her temples and ruins: "he had had many a pleasant snooze amongst them!" Another dwelt on the scenes of Montezuma's sorrows, for it was there he had partaken of most savoury wild fowl,—and yet another hero knew but of Peru and Pizarro's triumphs, by the markets producing very good prawns; whilst I must plead guilty to associating Greenland and the deeds of Scandinavian heroes with Herr Agar's seal-skin trowsers.

Amidst a last flourish of coals and dust, which left us filled to repletion,—indeed we were just awash,—we were ordered to take the ships in tow, and start. This being done, I came to a virtuous resolution in my own mind, after what I was going through in dragging my "fat friend," the "Resolute," about, to think twice ere I laughed at those whom fate had shackled to a mountain of flesh. When I had time to ask the day and date, it was Sunday, 28th June, 1850, and we had turned our back on the last trace of civilized man. Vogue-la-galère.

The night was serenely calm. We skirted the Black Land of Lively, making an average speed of three miles per hour, so that our fearful load of coal—full three hundred tons—did not diminish the speed nearly as much as I at first anticipated. Although I could not but feel from our staggering motion and bad steerage that the poor "Pioneer" was severely taxed in carrying her own dead weight of about five hundred tons, and towing a clumsy craft, which fully equalled another seven hundred tons, all this receiving vitality from two little engines of thirty-horse power each.

Whilst a sudden and rattling breeze from the south caused us to make sail and run merrily past the striking clifts of the Waigat and Jacob's Sound, I will briefly refer to the character of the vessels composing our squadrou, their equipment, and general efficiency.

The "Resolute" and "Assistance" were sailing ships rigged as barks; their hulls strengthened according to the most orthodox arctic rules, until, instead of presenting the appearances of a body intended for progress through the water, they resembled nothing so much as very ungainly snuff boxes; and their bows formed a buttress which rather pushed the water before it than passed through it. The remark made by an old seaman who had grown gray amongst the ice was often recalled to my mind, as with an aching heart for many a long mile I dragged the clumsy "Resolute" about. "Lord, sir! you would think by the quantity of wood they are putting into *them* ships, that the dock-yard maties believed they could stop the Almighty from moving the floes in Baffin's Bay! Every pound of African oak they put into them the less likely they are to rise to pressure; and you must in the ice either rise or sink. If the floe cannot pass through the ship it will go over it."

Internally the fittings of the ships were most perfect: nothing had been spared to render them the most comfortable vessels that ever went out avowedly to winter in the Polar ice. Hot air was distributed by means of an ingenious apparatus throughout lower deck and cabins. Double bulkheads and doors prevented the ingress of unnecessary cold air. A cooking battery, as the French say, promised abundance of room for roasting, boiling, baking, and thawing snow to make water for daily consumption. The mess places of the crew were neatly fitted in man-of-war style; and the well-laden shelves of crockery and hardware showed that Jack, as well as jolly marine, had spent a portion of his money in securing his comfort in the long voyage before them. A long tier of cabins on either side showed how large a proportion of officers these vessels carried; but it was so far satisfactory, as it proved that the division of labour, consequent upon numbers, would make arctic labours comparatively light.

A large captain's cabin, with a gunroom capable of containing all the officers when met together for their meals, completed the accommodation. The crews consisted of sixty souls each, of which a fourth were officers.

The vessels chosen to be the first to carry the novel agent, steam, into hyperborean climes, were the "Pioneer" and "Intrepid," sister vessels, belonging, originally, to the cattle conveyance company; they were propelled by screws, and were of sixty-horse power each, about 150 feet long, of 400 tons burden, and rigged as three-masted schooners. Over the whole of their original frames, tough planking called doubling was placed, varying from three to six inches in thickness. The decks were likewise doubled; and, as may be supposed, from such numerous fastenings passing through the original timbers of a merchantman, every timber was perforated with so many holes as to be weakened and rendered useless; indeed, the vessels may have at last been considered as what is termed "bread-and-butter built," the two layers of planking constituting with the decks the actual strength of the vessels. At the bow, the fine form had happily been retained, the timber strengthenings being thrown into them at that point within, and not without; they were, therefore, at the fore end somewhat like a strong wedge. Many an oracle had shaken his head at this novelty; and when I talked of cutting and breaking ice with an iron stem, the lip curled in derision and pity, and I saw that they thought of me as Joe Stag, the Plymouth boatman, did of the Brazilian frigate when she ran the breakwater down in a fog, —"Happy beggar, he knows nothing, and he fears nothing."

A few catastrophe-lovers in England having consigned Franklin to death because he had steam-engines and screws, every precaution was taken to secure the "Pioneer" and "Intrepid" in such a way that screw, rudder, and sternpost might be torn off by the much-talked-of *bogie!*—the ice,—and the vessels still be left fit to swim. In the internal arrangements for meeting an arctic climate, we were on somewhat a similar plan to the ships,—some difficulties being presented by the large mass of cold iron machinery, which, of course, acted as a rapid refrigerator. For the voyage out, the men were confined to a little place in the bows of the vessel, and from thence to the cabins of the officers, all was coal: a dead weight of 260 tons being originally carried from England, which we increased to 300 tons at the Whale Islands. This, at an average consumption of seven tons *per diem*, would enable us *to tow the ships* 3000 *miles*, or, *steam alone*, *full* 5000 *miles*, carrying twelve or eighteen months' provision. The crew consisted of thirty souls, all told, of which five were officers,—namely, a lieutenant in command and a second master, as executive officers; an assistant surgeon, who zealously undertook the superintendence of the commissariat, both public and private, and two engineers, to look after the steam department. These occupied the smallest conceivable space in the after-end of the steamers; and, with separate cabins, had a common mess-place.

Such were the arctic screws: it only remains for me to say, that they were very handsome, smart-sailing vessels, and those embarked in them partook of none of the anxieties and croakings, which declared opponents and doubtful allies entertained as to their success in what was styled a great experiment. They had but one wish ungratified, which was, that they had been sent alone and fully provisioned, instead of carrying an inadequate proportion of food, so that, in the event of being separated from the ships by accident, they might have wintered without suffering and hardship.

All the crews had been carefully chosen for health and efficiency; and they, as well as the officers, were actuated by the loftiest feelings of enterprise and humanity; and that feeling was fostered and strengthened by the knowledge they had, of the high confidence placed in the squadron by their country, speaking through the press. In fact, we were called heroes long before we had earned our laurels. Lastly, the Admiralty put into the hands of the officers the orders they had given the leader of this noble squadron; and there was but one opinion as to these orders, that more liberal, discretionary ones never were penned!—and with such power to act as circumstances might render necessary, we felt confident of deserving, if we could not demand, success.

June 24th, Baffin's Bay.—The squadron was flying north, in an open sea, over which bergs of every size and shape floated in wild magnificence. The excitement, as we dashed through the storm, in steering clear of them, was delightful from its novelty. Hard a starboard! Steady! Port! Port! you may!—and we flew past some huge mass, over which the green seas were fruitlessly trying to dash themselves. Coleridge describes the scene around us too well for me to degrade it with my prose. I will give his version:—

"And now there came both mist and snow,
And it grew wondrous cold,
And ice, mast high, came floating by
As green as emerald.
Through the drifts, the snowy clifts
Did send a dismal sheen;
Nor shapes of men, or beasts we ken,
The ice was all between.
With sloping masts, and dipping prow,
As who pursued with yell and blow,
Still treads the shadow of his foe,
And forward bends his head.
The ship drove fast—loud roared the blast,
And *northward* aye we fled—

Until we all suddenly hauled-in for the land of Greenland, in order to visit the settlement of Uppernavik. Passing into a channel, some four miles in width, we found ourselves running past the remarkable and lofty cliffs of "Sanderson his Hope," a quaint name given to this point by the "righte worthie Master Davis," in honour of his patron, a merchant of Bristol. Well worthy was it of one whose liberality had tended to increase our geographical knowledge; and the Hope's lofty crest pierced through the clouds which drove athwart its breast, and looked afar to see "whether the Lord of the Earth came not."

Under its lee, the water was a sheet of foam and spray, from the fierce gusts which swept down ravine and over headland; and against the base of the rocks, flights of wild fowl marked a spot famous amongst arctic voyagers as abounding in fresh food,—a charming variety to salt horse and Hambro' pork.

On rounding an inner islet of the Women's Group, as it is called, a straggling assemblage of Esquimaux huts, with a black and red storehouse or two, as at Disco, denoted the northernmost of the present Danish settlements, as well as the site of an ancient Scandinavian port,—a fact assured by the recent discovery of a stone pillar on one of the adjacent islands bearing the following inscription:—

"Elling Sigvatson, Bjame Thordason, and Endride Oddson, erected these memorial stones and cleared this place on Saturday before Gagndag (25th April), in the year 1135."

Exactly four hundred and fifty-two years before the place was rediscovered by our countryman, Davis.

The "Intrepid" having the honour of carrying-in the two post-captains, we box-hauled about in the offing until she returned with the disagreeable intelligence that all the English whalers were blocked up by ice, some thirty miles to the northward. Capt. Penny had been unable to advance, and the season was far from a promising one! Squaring our yards, we again bore up for the northward. In a few hours, a strong reflected light to the westward and northward showed we were fast approaching the ice-fields or floes of Baffin's Bay. A whaler, cruising about, shortly showed herself.

June 26th, 1850.—My rough notes are as follows:—A. M. Standing in for the land, northward of "Women's Isles," saw several whalers fast to the ice, inshore. Observe one of them standing out. H. M. S. "Assistance" is ordered to communicate. We haul to the wind. I visit the "Resolute." Learn that we altered course last night because the floes were seen extending across ahead. The whaler turns out to be the "Abram," Captain Gravill. He reports:—"Fourteen whalers stopped by the ice; Captain Penny, with his ships, after incurring great risk, and going through much severe labour, was watching the floes with the hope of slipping past them into the north water."

Mr. Gravill had lately ranged along the Pack edge as far south as Disco, and found not a single opening except the bight, up which we had been steering last night. He said, furthermore, "that there would be no passage across the bay, this year, for the whalers, because the water would not make sufficiently early to enable them to reach the fishing-ground in Pond's Bay by the first week in August; after which date, the whales travel southward towards Labrador." The report wound up with the discouraging statement that the whalemen agreed that the floes, this season, were unusually extensive, that the leads or cracks of water were few, and icebergs more numerous than they had been for some years.

It appears that a northerly gale has been blowing, with but slight intermission, for the last month; and that, in consequence, there is a large body of water to the north, the ice from which has been forced into the throat of Davis' Straits. All we have to pray for is, a continuation of the same breeze, for otherwise southerly winds will jam the whole body of it up in Melville Bay, and make what is called a "closed season."

Mr. G—— (though not a friend of Penny's) told us that Penny was working day and night to get ahead, and had already run no small risk, and undergone extraordinary labour. Poor Penny! I felt that fate had been against him! He deserved better than to be overtaken by us, after the energy displayed in the equipment of his squadron.

In the first watch the brigs "Lady Franklin" and "Sophia" were seen by us, fast between loose floe pieces, to seaward of which we continued to flirt. The "Intrepid" and "Pioneer" were now to be seen slyly trying their bows upon every bit of ice we could get near, without getting into a scrape with the commodore; and, from the ease with which they cut through the rotten stuff around our position, I already foresaw a fresh era in arctic history, and that the fine bows would soon beat the antediluvian "bluffs" out of the field.

Thursday, 27th June, 1850, found us still cruising about under canvas; northward and westward a body of dirty ice, fast decaying under a fierce sunlight, bergs in hundreds in every direction; and, dotted along the Greenland shore, a number of whalers fast in what is called "Land water," ready to take the first opening. The barometer falling, we were ordered to make fast to icebergs, every one choosing his own. This operation is a very useful one in arctic regions, and saves much unnecessary wear and tear of men and vessel, when progress in the required direction is no longer possible.

The bergs, from their enormous depth, are usually aground, except at spring-tides, and the seaman thus succeeds in anchoring his vessel in 200 fm. water, without any other trouble than digging a hole in the iceberg, placing an anchor in it called an ice-anchor, which one man can lift, and, with a whale-line, his ship rides out under the lee of this natural breakwater, in severe gales, and often escapes being beset in a lee pack.

Fastening to a berg has its risks and dangers; sometimes the first stroke of the man setting the ice-anchor, by its concussion causes the iceberg to break up, and the people so employed run great risk of being injured; at another time, vessels obliged to make fast under the steep side of a berg, have had pieces detach themselves from overhead, and injure materially the vessel and spars; and, again, the projecting masses, called tongues (which form under water the base of the berg), have been known to break off, and strike a vessel so severely as to sink her: all these risks are duly detailed by every arctic navigator, and the object always is, in fastening to an iceberg, to look for a side which is low and sloping, without any tongues under water. To such an one the Intrepid and Pioneer made fast, although the boat's crew that first reached it, in making a hole, were wetted by a projecting mass detaching itself with the first blow of the seaman's crowbar. A gale sprang up almost immediately, and during the night the Assistance blew adrift. Next day it abated, and the ice to the northward looked open.

In the evening one of Penny's vessels, the Sophia, joined us, and from her commander we soon heard of their hopes and disappointment. Directly after leaving Disco they fell in with the ice, and had fought their way the whole distance to their present position. The season was not promising, but forty-eight hours of a N. E. wind would do wonders, and I cordially partook of his opinion, that " keeping the vessel's nose to the crack" was the only way to get ahead in the arctic regions. The crews of the brigs were in rattling health and spirits. Having delivered him some letters and a number of parcels which, by great good luck, had not been landed at Uppernavik, Capt. Stewart returned to his chief, some eight miles northward of us, and we remained to watch progress.

Saturday, June 29th, 1850.—

Monday, July 1st, 1850.—At last the hoped-for signal, "take ships in tow," was made; and, with a leaping heart, we entered the lead, having the "Resolute" fast by the nose with a six-inch hawser. What looked impassable at ten miles' distance was an open lead when close to. Difficulties vanish when they are faced; and the very calm which rendered the whalers unable to take advantage of a loose pack, was just the thing for steamers. Away we went! past berg, past floe, winding in and out quietly, yet steadily!—and the whalers were soon astern. Penny, indefatigable, was seen struggling along the shore, with his boats ahead, towing, and every stitch of sail set to catch the lightest cat's paw: him too, however, we soon passed. The water ahead increased as we advanced, and we found, as is well known to be the case, that the pack-edge is always the tightest part of it.

Several whale-boats from the vessels astern were busy taking ducks' eggs from the islands, which seem to abound along the coast. When passing one of these islands that appeared remarkably steep, I was disagreeably surprised to feel the "Pioneer" strike against a sunken rock with some violence; she slipped off it, and then the "Resolute" gave herself a blow, which seemed to make every thing quiver again. Capt. Penny had a signal up warning us of the danger; but we were too busy to see it until afterwards, and then the want of wind prevented our ascertaining what was meant. After this accident we went very cautiously until the evening hour, when, having neared Cape Shackleton, and some thin ice showing itself, through which, at reduced speed, we could not tow the broad-bowed "Resolute," she was cast off, and made fast to some land ice, and I proceeded on alone in the "Pioneer" to see what the prospect was further on.

Cutting through some rotten ice of about six inches in thickness, we reached water beyond it, and saw a belt of water, of no great width, extending along shore as far as the next headland, called Horse's-head. Picking up a boat belonging to the "Chieftain" whaler, which had been shooting and egging, I returned towards the "Resolute" with my intelligence, giving Cape Shackleton a close shave to avoid the ice which was setting against it from the westward, the whalemen whom I had on board expressing no small astonishment and delight at the way in which we screwed through the broken ice of nine-inch thickness. On reaching the squadron, I found it made fast for the night, and parties of officers preparing to start in different directions to shoot, and see what was to be seen, for, of course, our night was as light as the day of any other region.

To the "Chieftain's" doctor I, with others of the "Pioneer," consigned what we flattered ourselves were our last letters, thinking that, now the steamers had got ahead, it was not likely the whalers would again be given an opportunity of communicating or overtaking us.

There is something in last letters painful and choking; and I remember that I hardly knew which feeling most predominated in my breast,—sorrow and regret for those friends I had left behind me, or hope and joyful anticipation of meeting those before us in the "Erebus and Terror."

At any rate, I gave vent to them by climbing the rocky summit of Cape Shackleton, and throwing off my jacket, let the cold breeze allay the excitement of my mind.

Nothing strikes the traveller in the north more strongly than the perceptible repose of Nature, although the sun is still illumining the heavens, during those hours termed night. We, of course, who were unaccustomed to the constant light, were restless and unable to sleep; but the inhabitants of these regions, as well as the animals, retire to rest with as much regularity as is done in more southern climes; and the subdued tints of the heavens, as well as the heavy banking of clouds in the neighbourhood of the sun, gives to the arctic summer night a quietude as marked as it is pleasant. Across Baffin's Bay there was ice! ice! ice! on every side, small faint streaks of water here and there in the distance, with one cheering strip of it winding snake-like along the coast as far as eye could reach. "To-morrow!" I exclaimed, "we will be there." "Yes!" replied a friend, "but if the breeze freshens, Penny will reach it to-night!" And there, sure enough, were Penny's brigs sailing past our squadron, which showed no sign of vitality beyond that of the officer of the watch visiting the ice-anchors to see all was right. "That fellow, Penny, is no sluggard!" we muttered, "and will yet give the screws a hard tussle to beat him."

A couple of hours rest, and having taken the ship in tow, we again proceeded, and at about seven o'clock on the morning of the 2d of July passed the "Sophia," and shortly afterwards, the "Lady Franklin." Alas! poor Penny, he had a light contrary wind to work against.

I do not think my memory can recall in the course of my wanderings any thing more novel or striking than the scenes through which we steamed this forenoon. The land of Greenland, so bold, so steep, and in places so grim, with the long fields of white glittering ice floating about on the cold blue sea, and our little vessels (for we looked pigmies beside the huge objects around us, whether cliff, berg, or glacier) stealing on so silently and quickly; the leadsman's song or the flap of wild fowl the only sounds to break the general stillness. One of the cliffs we skirted along was actually teeming with birds called "loons:" they might have been shot in tens of hundreds had we required them or time not pressed: they are considered remarkably good eating, and about the size and weight of an ordinary duck: to naturalists they are known by the name of guillemot, and were christened "loons" by the early Dutch navigators, in consequence of their stupidity. Numerous seals lay on the ice in the offing, and their great size astonished us.

As we advanced, a peculiarly conical island, in a broad and ice-encumbered bay, showed itself: it was "the Sugar-Loaf Island" of the whalers; and told us that, on rounding the farther headland, we should see the far-famed Devil's Thumb, the boundary of Melville Bay.

A block of ice brought us up after a tow of some twenty-five or thirty miles, and, each vessel picking up a convenient iceberg, we made fast to await an opening.

I landed to obtain a view from a small islet close to the "Pioneer," and was rewarded by observing that the Duck Islands, a group some fifteen miles to seaward of us, had evidently a large space of open water around them, and broad *lanes* extended from these in divers directions towards us, although, without retracing our steps, there was at present no direct road for us into this water.

Captain Penny, however, being astern, had struck to seaward, and was fast passing our position.

On the islands there were recent traces of both reindeer and bears; and I amused myself picking some pretty arctic flowers, such as anemones, poppies, and saxifrage, which grew in sheltered nooks amongst the rocks.

Before leaving the vessel, a boat had been despatched to the headland where so many "loons" had been seen, to shoot for the ship's company's use: the other ships did likewise: they returned at about four o'clock next morning, and I was annoyed at being informed, without any birds, although all the powder and shot had been expended.

I sent for the captain of the forecastle, who had been away in charge of the sportsmen, and, with astonishment, asked how he had contrived to fire away one pound of powder and four of small shot, without bringing home some loons? Hanging his head, and looking uncommonly bashful, he answered, "If you please, sir, we fired it all into a bear!" "Into a bear?" I exclaimed, "what! shoot a bear with No. 4 shot?" "Yes, sir," replied Abbot; "and if it hadn't have been for two or three who were afeard of him, we would have brought him aboard, too." Sending my bear-hunting friend about his business for neglecting my orders to obtain fresh food for the crew, I afterward found out that on passing a small island between the "Pioneer" and the Loon Head, as the cliff was called, my boat's crew had observed a bear watching some seals, and it was voted immediately, that to be the first to bring a bear home, would immortalize the "Pioneer."

A determined onslaught was therefore made on Bruin: No. 4 shot being poured into him most ruthlessly, he growled and snapped his teeth, trotted round the island, and was still followed and fired at, until, finding the fun all on one side, the brute plunged into the water, and swam for some broken-up ice; my heroes followed, and, for lack of ball, fired at him a waistcoat button and the blade of a knife, which, by great ingenuity, they had contrived to cram down one of their muskets; this very naturally, as they described it, "made the beast jump again!" he reached the ice, however, bleeding all over, but not severely injured; and whilst the bear was endeavouring to get on the floe, a spirited contest ensued between him and Old Abbot, the latter trying to become possessor of a skin, which the former gallantly defended.

Ammunition expended, and nothing but boat-hooks and stretchers left as defensive weapons, there seemed some chance of the tables being reversed, and the boat's crew very properly obliged the captain of the forecastle to beat a retreat; the bear, equally well pleased to be rid of such visitors, made off. "Old Abbot," as he was styled, always, however, asserted, that if he had had his way, the bear would have been brought on board the "Pioneer," and tamed to do a good deal of the dragging work of the sledges; and whenever he heard, in the winter, any of the young hands growling at the labour of sledging away snow or ice, he created a roar of laughter, by muttering, "Ah! if you had taken my advice, we'd have had that 'ere bear to do this work for us!"

July 3d, 1850.—Penny, by taking another route, gave us the "go by," and in the afternoon we started, taking an in-shore lane of water. The wind, however, had freshened up from the westward, and as we advanced, the ice was rapidly closing, the points of the floe-pieces forming "bars," with holes of water between them. With the "Pioneer's" sharp bow, we broke through the first of these barriers, and carried the "Resolute" into "a hole of water," as it is called. The next bar being broader, I attempted to force it by charging with the steamer, and after breaking up a portion of it, backed astern to allow the broken pieces to be removed; this being the first time this operation was performed, and much having to be learnt upon the feasibility of the different modes of applying steam-power against ice.

We soon found ourselves surrounded with broken masses, which, owing to the want of men to remove it away into the open water astern, rendered advance or retreat, without injury to the propeller, almost impossible. Here the paucity of men on board the steam vessels was severely felt: for until the "Resolute" was properly secured I could expect no assistance from her; and the "Pioneer," therefore, had to do her best with half the number of men, although she was fifty feet longer than the ship. Unable to move, the closing floes fast beset the steamer, and then the large parties of men that joined from the squadron to assist were useless, beyond some practice, which all seemed willing to undertake, in the use of ice-tools, consisting of chisels, poles with iron points, claws, lines, &c.

In a short time, the prospect of liberating the "Pioneer" was seen to be farcical, and all the officers and men from the "Resolute" returned to their ship, although parties of novices would walk down constantly to see the first vessel beset in the ice.

A few birds playing about induced myself and some others to go out shooting, a foggy night promising to be favourable to our larders. The ice, however, was full of holes, and very decayed; in addition to which it was in rapid motion in many places, from the action of wind and tide. The risk of such sporting was well evinced in my gallant friend M——'s case. He was on one side of a lane of water, and I on the other: a bird called a "Burgomaster" flew over his head to seaward, and he started in the direction it had gone. I and another shouted to warn him of the ice being in rapid motion and very thin; he halted for a moment, and then ran on, leaping from piece to piece. The fog at this moment lifted a little, and most providentially so, for suddenly I saw M—— make a leap and disappear—the ice had given way!—he soon rose, but without his gun, and I then saw him scramble upon a piece of ice, and on watching it, observed with a shudder that both he and it were drifting to the northward, and away from us. Leaving my remaining companion to keep sight of M——, and thus to point out the way on my return, I retraced my steps to the "Pioneer," and with a couple of men, a long hand-line, and boarding-pikes, started off in the direction M—— was in.

I could tell my route pretty well by my companion's voice, which in rich Milesian was giving utterance to encouraging exclamations of the most original nature—"Keep up your courage, my boy!—Why don't you come back?—Faith, I suppose it's water that won't let you!—There will be some one there directly!—Hoy! hoy! ahoy! don't be downhearted anyway!" I laughed as I ran. My party placed themselves about ten yards apart, the last man carrying the line, ready to heave, in case of the leader breaking through. So weak was the ice that we had to keep at a sharp trot to prevent the weight of our own bodies resting long on any one spot; and when we sighted our friend M—— on his little piece of firm ice, the very natural exclamation of one of my men was, "I wonder how he ever reached it, sir?" M—— assisted us to approach him by pointing out his own route; and by extending our line, and holding on to it, we at last got near enough to take him off the piece of detached ice on which he had providentially scrambled. I never think of the occurrence without a sickening sensation, mixed with a comic recollection of K——'s ejaculations. Whilst walking back with my half-frozen friend, the ice showed itself to be easing off rapidly with the turn of tide. At 1 A. M. we were all free, and a lane of water extending itself ahead.

July 4th.—At 1 P. M. we started again, towing the ships, the whaling fleet from the southward under every stitch of canvas threatening to reach the Duck Islands before ourselves, and Captain Penny's squadron out of sight to the north-west. By dint of hard steaming we contrived to reach the islands before the whalers, and at midnight got orders to cast off and cruise about under sail, all the vessels rejoining us that we had passed some days ago off the Women's Isles.

The much talked of, by whalemen, "Devil's Thumb," was now open; it appears to be a huge mass of granite or basalt, which rears itself on a cliff of some 600 or 800 feet elevation, and is known as the southern boundary of Melville Bay, round whose dreary circuit, year after year, the fishermen work their way to reach the large body of water about the entrance of Lancaster Sound and Pond's Bay. Facing to the south-west, from whence the worst gales of wind at this season of the year arise, it is not to be wondered at that Melville Bay has been the grave of many a goodly craft, and in one disastrous year the whaling fleet was diminished by no less than twenty-eight sail (without the loss of life, however), a blow from which it never has recovered. No good reason was adduced for taking this route, beyond the argument, founded upon experience, that the earliest passages were always to be made by Melville Bay; this I perfectly understood, for early in the season, when northerly winds do prevail, the coast of Melville Bay is a weather-shore, and the ice, acted upon by wind and current, would detach itself and form between the land-ice and the pack-ice a safe high-road to the westward. It was far otherwise in 1850. The prospect of an early passage, viz., from the first to the third week of June, had long vanished. Southerly winds, after so long a prevalence of northerly ones (vide Captain Gravill's information), were to be expected. The whole weight of the Atlantic would be forced up Davis's Straits, and Melville Bay become "a dead lee-shore." I should therefore not have taken the ice, or attempted to work my way round Melville Bay, and would instead have gone to the westward and struck off sooner or later into the west water, in about the latitude of Uppernavik, 73° 30′ N.

However, this is what amongst the experienced is styled theory; and as any thing was better than standing still, I was heartily glad to see the "Chieftain," a bonnie Scotch whaler, show us the road by entering a lead of water, and away we all went, working to windward. The sailing qualities of the naval Arctic ships threatened to be sadly eclipsed by queer-looking craft, like the "Truelove" and others. But steam came to the rescue, and after twelve hours' hard struggle we got the pendants again ahead of our enterprising and energetic countrymen.

. . . . . .

Saturday, July 6th.—By 6 A. M. we were alongside of Penny's squadron, which was placed at the head of the lane of water, up which we had also advanced; and so keen was he not to lose the post of honour, that as we closed, I smiled to see the Aberdonians move their vessels up into the very "nip." In the course of the day the whalers again caught us up, and a long line of masts and hulls dotted the floe-edge.

The ice was white and hard, affording good exercise for pedestrians, and to novices, of whom there were many amongst us, the idea of walking about on the frozen surface of the sea was not a little charming. In all directions groups of three and four persons were seen trudging about, and the constant puffs of smoke which rose in the clear atmosphere, showed that shooting for the table was kept carefully in view.

A present of 170 duck-eggs from Captain Stewart of the

"Joseph Green" whaler, showed in what profusion these birds breed, and I was told by Captain Penny that one of the islets passed by him on the 2d was literally alive with ducks, and that several boat-loads of eggs might have been taken off it,—interesting proofs of the extraordinary abundance of animal life in these northern regions. Our Saturday evening was passed listening to stirring tales of Melville Bay and the whale fishery, and several prophecies as to the chances of a very bad season, the number of icebergs and extent of the ice-fields, inducing many to believe that more than usual risk would be run in the bay this year. Sunday forenoon passed quietly and according to law, though a falling barometer made us watch anxiously a heavy bank of black clouds which rested in the southern heavens.

The dinner-bell however rang, and having a very intelligent gentleman who commands a whaler as a guest, we were much interested in listening to his description of the strange life led by men, like himself, engaged in the adventurous pursuit of the whale; Mr. S. assured us that he had not seen corn grow, or eaten fresh gooseberries for thirty years! although he had been at home every winter. Though now advanced in years, with a large family, one of whom was the commander of Her Majesty's brig the "Sophia," then in company, still he spoke with enthusiasm of the excitement and risks of his own profession; it had its charms for the old sailor, whose skill and enterprise had been excited for so many years in braving the dangers of ice-encumbered seas, whether around Spitzbergen or in Baffin's Bay: he evidently felt a pride and satisfaction in his past career, and it had still sweet reminiscences for him. I felt a pride in seeing such a man a brother-seaman,—one who loved the North because it had hardships—one who delighted to battle with a noble foe. "We are the only people," he said, "who follow the whale, and kill him in spite of the ice and cold." There was the true sportsman in such feelings. He and the whale were at war, —not even the ice could save his prey.

A report from deck, that the ice was coming in before a southerly gale, finished our dinner very abruptly, and the alteration that had taken place in a couple of hours was striking. A blue sky had changed to one of a dusky colour, —a moaning gale sent before it a low brown vapour, under which the ice gleamed fiercely,—the floes were rapidly pressing together. Two whalers were already nipped severely, and their people were getting the boats and clothing out ready for an accident.

"The sooner we are all in dock the better," said Captain S., as he hurried away to get his own vessel into safety, and, almost as quickly as I can tell it, a scene of exciting interest commenced—that of cutting docks in the fixed ice, called land-floe, so as to avoid the pressure which would occur at its edge by the body of ice to seaward being forced against it by the fast rising gale. Smart things are done in the Navy, but I do not think any thing could excel the alacrity with which the floe was suddenly peopled by about 500 men, triangles rigged, and the long saws (called ice-saws) used for cutting

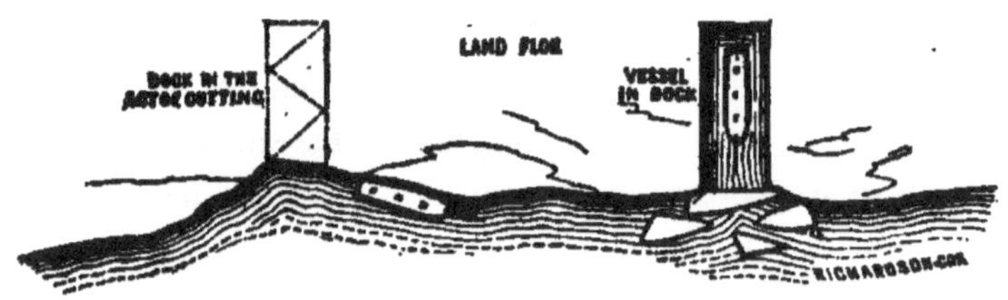

the ice, were manned. A hundred songs from hoarse throats resounded through the gale; the sharp chipping of the saws told that the work was flying; and the loud laugh or broad witticisms of the crews mingled with the words of command and encouragement to exertion given by the officers.

The pencil of a Wilkie could hardly convey the characteristics of such a scene, and it is far beyond my humble pen to tell of the stirring animation exhibited by some twenty ships' companies, who knew that on their own exertions depended the safety of their vessels and the success of their voyage. The ice was of an average thickness of three feet, and to cut this saws of ten feet long were used, the length of stroke being about as far as the men directing the saw could reach up and down. A little powder was used to break up the pieces that were cut, so as to get them easily out of the mouth of the dock, an operation which the officers of our vessels performed whilst the men cut away with the saws. In a very short time all the vessels were in safety, the pressure of the pack expending itself on a chain of bergs some ten miles north of our present position. The unequal contest between floe and iceberg exhibited itself there in a fearful manner; for the former pressing onward against the huge grounded masses was torn into shreds, and thrown back piecemeal, layer on layer of many feet in elevation, as if mere shreds of some flimsy material, instead of solid, hard ice, every cubic yard of which weighed nearly a ton.

The smell of our numerous fires brought a bear in sight; Nimrods without number issued out to slay him, the weapons being as varied as the individuals were numerous. The chase would, however, have been a fruitless one, had not the bear in his retreat fallen in with and killed a seal; his voracity overcame his fears, and being driven into the water, he was shot from the boat of one of the whalers which had perseveringly followed him.

The brute was of no great size—not more than five feet in

length. The coat, instead of being white, was turned to a dingy yellow, much resembling in colour decayed ice; a resemblance which enabled the animal, no doubt, to approach the seals with greater facility.

By midnight all fears for the safety of the vessels had ceased; indeed, as far as our searching ships had been concerned, there never had been much cause for fear, the operation of docking having been carried out by us more for the sake of practice than from necessity. We were tightly beset until the following evening, when the ice as suddenly moved off as it had come together; and then a scene of joyful excitement took place, such as is only to be seen in the arctic regions—every ship striving to be foremost in her escape from imprisonment, and to lead ahead. Want of wind obliged the whalers and Penny's brigs to be tracked along the floe-edge by the crews—a laborious operation, which is done on our English canals by horses; here, however, the powerful crews of fishermen, mustering from thirty-five to fifty hands, fastened on by their track-belts to a whale-line, and, with loud songs, made their vessels slip through the water at an astonishing pace.

An odd proof of the unhandiness of such vessels as the "Resolute" and "Assistance" was given to-day: the former endeavoured to tow herself ahead by the aid of all her boats, a distance of about three or four hundred yards, and was quite unable to do so, although the wind against her hardly amounted to a cat's paw; the consequence was, that until the steam vessels got hold, she was fast dropping astern of the whalers, and, as was usually the case, every one's temper was going wrong. The run was not a very long one, and in the heart of a fleet of icebergs we again brought up: one whaler, "The Truelove," having turned back in despair of a passage north-about to Pond's Bay.

From our position a good view of Melville Bay was to be had, and a more melancholy one, eye never rested upon. Surrounded as we were with bergs, we had to climb a neighbouring mass to obtain a clear horizon; the prospect to seaward was not cheering; and from the Devil's Thumb northward, one huge glacier spread itself. The first sensation we felt was that of pity for the poor land—pressed down and smothered under so deadly a weight: here and there, a strip of cliff protruded, black and bare, from the edge of the *mer-de-glace*, whose surface, rough and unpleasing, was of a sombre yellowish tint, with occasional masses of basalt protruding through it, like the uplifted hands of drowning men: it seemed Earth's prayer for light and life; but the ice, shroud-like, enveloped it, and would not give up the dead.

July 9th.—Every day taught us something: we had learned that the ice went off as rapidly, if not more so, than it came in; and when an opening occurred to-day, the "Pioneer," with the "Resolute" again in tow, was ahead of the whalers, and close on Penny's heels.

The ice to-day lay much across, forming very tortuous channels; and the performance of the screws, in twisting themselves and their tail-pieces (the ships) round floe-pieces and bergs, was as interesting as it was satisfactory. In some places we had to adopt a plan, styled by us "making a cannon!" from its resemblance to the same feat in billiards. This generally occurred at sharp and intricate turns, where the breadth of water was considerably less than the length of the vessels; we then, in order to get the vessel's stem in the proper direction, used to steer her in such a way, that the bow on the opposite side to which we wanted her to turn struck the ice with some force; the consequence was, the steamer would turn short off, and save the risk of getting athwart "the lead," and aid in checking the ship round at the same time.

Another novel application of steam took place to-day. We came to a bar of ice, formed of loose floe-pieces of all sizes, but too small to heave through by means of ice-anchors and lines; Penny stood close up to it, but he could neither sail through it, nor warp; he had therefore to make a long detour round its edge: *steam* however was able to do it; and with our knife-like bows, aided by the propeller, we soon wedged a road through for ourselves and the "Resolute."

Detentions in the ice were amongst the most trying moments of our life in the North; and from the composition of our squadron, namely, two fast vessels, and two slow ones, the constant waiting for one another put me much in mind of the old doggerel:—

"The Earl of Chatham with sword drawn,
Was waiting for Sir Richard Strachan;
Sir Richard longing to be at 'em,
Was waiting for the Earl of Chatham."

The risk of detention in such a region can be understood by all; but few, perhaps, will appreciate the feeling of mingled passion and regret with which the leading vessel in such a mission as we had in hand found herself obliged to wait to close her consort, when all was water ahead, and the chances of it remaining so were but slight. A few hours we all knew had often made the difference of a passage across Melville Bay without detention, or of a long, laborious voyage —here we were waiting for our consorts.

On the 10th, a short tow; and in company with a portion of the whalers, for several had retreated, we again had to dock, to escape nipping from the ice, and on the morrow, a similar scene of hurry and excitement took place when liberation came.

Thursday, 11*th*.—Seven of the most enterprising whalers still hung on our heels, and to-day found us all at a bar beyond which there was a sea of water. Patience! was the "*mot d'ordre*;" and it vented itself in a number of dinners and the winding-up of letters; for we all felt that the hour of separation from the whalers would soon arrive. They all were delighted with the performance of the steam vessels in the ice, and quizzed our crews for sitting at their ease, whilst they had to drag like horses. Captain Penny, likewise, candidly acknowledged that he never thought they could have answered so well; and regretted that he had not had a steam vessel. Our seamen fully appreciated the good service the screws had done them: they had now been eleven days in the ice, during every day of which period they had witnessed it working effectually under every circumstance; they had seen the crews of the whalers labouring at the track-line, at the oar, and in making and shortening sail, both by day and by night; whilst our crews had nothing to do beyond taking the ships in tow and casting them off again; already I observed a really sincere anxiety upon all their parts for the safety of the "screw." I heard from henceforth inquiries amongst them, whenever a shock took place, "Whether *she* was all right?" or to my orders, a ready response—"All right, sir! she is all free of the ice!"

At night the bar opened, and giving the "Lady Franklin" a jerk into the water beyond, the "Intrepid" and "Pioneer" rattled away with the ships in tow, as hard as steam could take them. Oh, for one run of ninety miles! There was open water ahead; but, alas! we could only get three miles an hour out of our vessel—alone, we could have gone five;

making in a day's work the difference between seventy-two and one hundred and twenty miles.

By two o'clock in the morning we had outrun both Penny and the whalers; and, could we only have gone faster, assuredly the passage of Melville Bay would have been that day effected. The land-floe was still fast, reaching twenty-five or thirty miles off shore, and the pack had drifted off some ten or fifteen miles; between the two we were steaming at five o'clock in the morning of the 12th of July, and all was promising—a headland called Cape Walker and Melville Monument opening fast to view. The quarter-master grinned, as he made his report, that he was sure we were in what was a fair lead into the North Water!

Hope is not prophecy! and so they will find who labour in the North; for how changed was the prospect when I went on deck after a short sleep—a south wind had sprung up. We were under sail. The pack was coming in fast, and the signal "Prepare to take the ice," flying from the Commodore's mast-head. We did take it, as the pack came against the land-floe, with Cape Walker about abreast of us; and, in a few hours, the "nip" took place. The "Intrepid" and "Pioneer" having gone into a natural dock together, were secure enough until the projecting points of the land-floe gave way, when the weight of the pressure came on the vessels, and then we felt, for the first time, a Melville Bay squeeze. The vessels, lifted by the floes, shot alternately ahead of one another, and rode down the floe for some fifty yards, until firmly imbedded in ice, which, in many layers, formed a perfect cradle under their bottoms. We, of course, were passive spectators, beyond taking the precaution to have a few men following the vessels over the ice with two or three of the boats, in case of a fatal squeeze. The "Sweet little Cherub" watched over the steamers, however, and, in a short time, the pressure transferred itself elsewhere. Next day showed all of Her Majesty's squadron beset in Melville Bay. The gale had abated, but an immense body of ice had come in from the S. W. To the N. W. a dark haze showed a water sky, but from it we must have been at least forty miles. Between us and the shore, a land-floe, of some thirty miles in width, followed the sinuosities of the coast-line. Bergs here and there strewed its surface; but the major part of them formed what is called a "reef," in the neighbourhood of Devil's Thumb, denoting either a bank or shoal water in that direction.

A powerful sunlight obliged spectacles of every shade, size, and description to be brought into use; and, as we walked about from ship to ship, a great deal of joking and facetiousness arose out of the droll appearance of some individuals,—utility, and not beauty, was, however, generally voted the great essential in our bachelor community; and good looks, by general consent, put away for a future day. Great reflection, as well as refraction, existed for the time we remained beset in this position; and the refraction on one occasion enabled us to detect Captain Penny's brigs as well as the whalers, although they must have been nearly thirty miles distant.

The ice slackening a little formed what are called "holes of water," and in these we soon observed a shoal of narwhales, or unicorn fish, to be blowing and enjoying themselves. By extraordinary luck, one of the officers of the "Intrepid," in firing at them, happened to hit one in a vital part, and the brute was captured; his horn forming a handsome trophy for the sportsman. The result of this was, that the unfortunate narwhales got no peace; directly they showed themselves, a shower of balls was poured into them.

This fish is found throughout the fishing-ground of Baffin's

Bay, but is not particularly sought for by our people. The Esquimaux kill it with ease, and its flesh and skin are eaten as luxuries; the latter especially, as an anti-scorbutic, even by the whalers, and some of our crews partook of the extremely greasy-looking substance,—one man vowing it was very like chestnuts! (?) I did not attempt to judge for myself; but I have no doubt it would form good food to a really hungry person. The narwhales vary in size, ranging sometimes, I am told, to fourteen feet; the horns, of which I saw a great many at Whale-Fish Isles, were from three feet to seven feet in length. The use of this horn is a matter of controversy amongst the fishermen: it is almost too blunt for offence, and its point, for about four inches, is always found well polished, whilst the remainder of it is usually covered with slime and greenish sea-weed. Some maintain that it roots up food from the bottom of the sea with this horn; others, that it probes the clefts and fissures of the floating ice with it, to drive out the small fish, which are said to be its prey, and which instinctively take shelter there from their pursuers. The body of the narwhale is covered with a layer of blubber, of about two inches in thickness. This was removed, and carefully boiled down to make oil; and the *krang*, or carcass, was left as a decoy to molliemauks and ivory-gulls,—these latter birds having for the first time been seen by me to-day. They are decidedly the most graceful of sea-birds; and, from the exquisite purity of their plumage when settled on a piece of ice or snow, it required a practised eye to detect them. Not so the voracious and impertinent mollies—the Procellaria of naturalists. Their very ugliness appeared to give them security, and they are, in the North, what the vulture and carrion crow are in more pleasant climes —Nature's scavengers.

The 14th and 15th of July found us still firmly beset, and

sorely was our patience taxed. In-shore of us, a firm unbroken sheet of ice extended to the land, some fifteen miles distant. Across it, in various directions, like hedge-rows in an English landscape, ran long lines of piled-up hummocks, formed during the winter by some great pressure; and on the surface, pools of water and sludge* broke the general monotony of the aspect.

The striking mass of rock, known as Melville's Monument, was clear of snow, because it was too steep for ice to adhere; but every where else huge domes of white showed where Greenland lay, except where Cape Walker thrust its black cliff through the glacier to scowl upon us.

Tantalus never longed for water more than we did. Those who have been so beset can alone tell of the watchfulness and headaching for water. Now to the mast-head with straining eyes,—then arguing and inferring, from the direction of wind and tide, that water must come. Others strolling over to a hole, and with fragments of wood, or a measure, endeavouring to detect that movement in the floes by which liberation was to be brought about. Some sage in uniform, perhaps, tries to prove, by the experience of former voyages, that the lucky day is passed or close at hand; whilst wiser ones console themselves with exclaiming, "That, at any rate, we are, as yet, before Sir James Ross's expedition,—both in time and position."

The 16th of July showed more favourable symptoms, and Captain Penny was seen working for a lane of water, a long way in-shore of us. In the night, a general disruption of the fixed ice was taking place in the most marvellous manner; and, by the next morning, there was nearly as much water as there had before been ice. The two steamers,

---

* Is the term applied to half-thawed ice or snow.

firmly imbedded in a mass of ice, many miles in circumfer ence, were drifting rapidly to the southward, whilst the two ships, afloat in a large space of water and fastened to the floe, awaited our liberation.

The prospect of a separation from the ships, when unavoidable, in no wise depressed the spirits of my colleague of the "Intrepid," nor myself. Like the man who lost a scolding wife, we felt if it must be so, it was for the best, and we were resigned. But it was not to be; the "Intrepid" with her screw, and the "Pioneer" with gunpowder, which, for the first time, was now applied, shook the fragments apart in which we were beset, and again we laid hold of our mentors. A thick fog immediately enveloped us, and in it we got perfectly puzzled, took a wrong lead, and, tumbling into a perfect *cul de sac*, made fast, to await a break in the weather. The 18th of July, from the same cause, a dense fog, was a lost day, and next day Penny again caught us up. He reported the whalers to have given up all idea of a Northern fishery this season. Alas! for the many friends who will be disappointed in not receiving letters! and alas! for the desponding, who will croak and sigh at the whalers failing to get across the bay, believing, therefore, that *we* shall fail likewise.

Penny had passed a long way inside of the spot the steamers had been beset and nipped in; and he witnessed a sight which, although constantly taking place, is seldom seen —the entire dissolution of an enormous iceberg.

This iceberg had been observed by our squadron, and remarked for its huge size and massiveness, giving good promise of resisting a century of sun and thaw. All on board the "Lady Franklin" described as a most wonderful spectacle this iceberg, without any warning, falling, as it were, to pieces; the sea around it resembled a seething caldron, from the violent plunging of the masses, as they broke and rebroke in a thousand pieces! The floes, torn up for a distance of ten miles by the violent action of the rollers, threatened, by the manner the ice was agitated, to destroy any vessel that had been amongst it; and they congratulated themselves, on being sufficiently removed from the scene of danger, to see without incurring any immediate risk.

The fog again lifted for a short time. Penny went in my "crow's nest," as well as into the "Resolute's," and soon gave us the disagreeable intelligence, that the land-floe had broken up, and we were in the pack, instead of having, as we had fancied, "fast ice" to hold on by; and, as he remarked, "We can do nothing but push for it;—it's all broken ice, and push we must, in-shore, or else away we go with the loose floes!"

With this feeling the six vessels started in the night, in an indifferent and cross lead, we towing the "Resolute" and "Lady Franklin,"—the "Intrepid," with "Assistance" and "Sophia," astern. Breaking through two light barriers of ice, the prospect was improving; and, as they said from the "crow's nest," that eight miles of water was beyond a neck of ice ahead, I cast off the vessel in tow to charge the ice; at first she did well, but the floe was nearly six feet thick, hard and sound, and a pressure on it besides. The "Pioneer" was again caught, and the squadron anchored to the floe to await an opening. A few hours afterwards we were liberated, and, moving the vessel as far astern as we could, the fact was duly reported to the senior officer; but, as the road ahead was not open, no change of position could be made. On the morning of the 20th we were again beset, and a south gale threatened to increase the pressure; escape was, however, impossible, and "Fear not, but trust in Providence" is a necessary motto for Arctic seamen. My faith in this axiom was soon put to the proof. After a short sleep I was called on deck, as the vessel was suffering from great pressure. My own senses soon made it evident; every timber and plank was cracking and groaning, the vessel was thrown considerably over on her side, and lifted bodily, the bulkheads cracking, and treenails and bolts breaking with small reports. On reaching the deck, I saw indeed that the poor "Pioneer" was in sad peril; the deck was arching with the pressure on her sides, the scupper-pieces were turning up out of the mortices, and a quiver of agony wrung my craft's frame from stem to taffrail, whilst the floe, as if impatient to overwhelm its victim, had piled up as high as the bulwark in many places.

The men who, whaler-fashion, had, without orders I afterwards learnt, brought their clothes on deck, ready to save their little property, stood in knots, waiting for directions from the officers, who, with anxious eye, watched the floe-edge as its ground passed the side, to see whether the strain was easing; suddenly it did so, and we were safe! But a deep dent in the "Pioneer's" side, extending for some forty feet, and the fact, as we afterwards learnt, of twenty-one timbers being broken upon one side, proved that her trial had been a severe one.

Again had the ice come in upon us from the S. W., and nothing but a steady, watchful progress through the pack was left to our squadron, as well as Penny's. But I shall not weary the reader with the dry detail of our every-day labours,—their success or futility. Keenly and anxiously did we take advantage of every move in the ice, between the 20th and 31st July, yet, not seven miles in the right direction was made good; the first of August found us doubting, considerably, the prospect of reaching Lancaster Sound by a northern passage; and Capt. Penny decided, if the water approached him from the south, to strike to the westward in a lower latitude.

The ships—generally the "Resolute"—kept the lead in our heaving and warping operation through the pack; and, leaving a small portion of the crews to keep the other vessels close up under her stern, the majority of the officers and men laboured at the headmost ship, to move her through the ice. Heaving ahead with stout hawsers, blasting with gunpowder, cutting with ice-saws, and clipping with ice-chisels, was perseveringly carried on; but the progress fell far short of the labour expended, and the bluff bow slipped away from the nip instead of wedging it open. Warping the "Resolute" through a barrier of ice by lines out of her hawse-holes, put me in mind of trying to do the same with a cask, by a line through the bung-hole: she slid and swerved every way but the right one, ahead; I often saw her bring dead up, as if a wall had stopped her. After a search, some one would exclaim, "Here is the piece that jams her!" and a knock with a two-pound chisel would bring up a piece of ice two or three inches thick! In short, all, or nearly all, of us soon learnt to see, that the fine bow was the one to get ahead in these regions; and the daily increasing advantage which Penny had over us, was a proof which the most obstinate could not dispute.

I often thought how proud our countrymen would be of their seamen, could they have looked on the scene of busy energy and activity displayed in the solitude of Melville Bay:—the hearty song, the merry laugh, and zealous labours of the crew; day after day the same difficulties to contend with, yet day after day met with fresh resolution and new resources; a wide horizon of ice, no sea in sight, yet every foot gained to the northward was talked of with satisfaction and delight; men and officers vieing with one another in laborious duties, the latter especially, finding amongst a body of seamen, actuated by such noble and enthusiastic feelings, no necessity to fear an infringement of their dignity. The etiquette of the quarter-deck was thrown on one side for the good of the common cause; and on every side, whether at the capstan, at the track-line, hauling, heaving, or cutting, the officer worked as hard as the seamen,—each was proud of the other, and discipline suffered nought, indeed improved: for here Jack had both precept and example.

If we had our labours, it is not to be wondered at that we had also our leisure and amusements, usually at night,—a polar night robed in light,—then, indeed, boys fresh from school never tossed care more to the winds than did the majority of us. Games, which men in any other class of society would vote childish, were entered into with a zest which neither gray hairs nor stout bodies in any degree had damped. Shouts of laughter! roars of "Not fair, not fair! run again!" "Well done, well done!" from individuals leaping and clapping their hands with excitement, arose from many a merry ring, in which "rounders," with a cruelly hard ball, was being played. In other directions the fiddle and clarionet were hard at work, keeping pace with heels which seemed likely never to cease dancing, evincing more activity than grace. Here a sober few were heaving quoits, there a knot of Solomons talked of the past, and argued as to the future, whilst in the distance the sentimental ones strolled about, thinking no doubt of some one's goodness and beauty, in honour of whom, like true knights, they had come thus far to win bright honour from the "Giant of the North."

Sometimes a bear would come in sight, and then his risk of being shot was not small, for twenty keen hands were out after the skin: it had been promised as a *gage d'amour* by one to his betrothed; to a sister by another; a third intended to open the purse-strings of a hard-hearted parent by such a proof of regard; and not a few were to go to the First Lord with it, in exchange for a piece of parchment, if he would not object to the arrangement.

Every day our sportsmen brought home a fair proportion of loons and little auks, the latter bird flying in immense flocks to all the neighbouring pools of water, and to kill ten or twelve of them at a shot when settled to feed, was not considered as derogatory to the character of a Nimrod, where the question was a purely gastronomic one. I found in my shooting excursions an India-rubber boat, constructed upon a plan of my dear friend Peter Halkett, to be extremely convenient; in it I floated down the cracks of water, landed on floe-pieces, crossed them dragging my boat, and again launched into water in search of my feathered friends. At the Whale-Fish Islands, much to the delight of my Esquimaux friends, I had paddled about in the inflated boat, and its portability seemed fully to be appreciated by them, though they found fault with the want of speed, in which it fell far short of their own fairy craft.

The separation of the squadron, occasioned by either mistake or accident, detained us for a few days in the beginning of August, in order that junction might again take place. Penny, by dint of hard tracking and heaving, gained seven miles upon us. For several days a schooner, a ketch, and a single-masted craft, had been seen far to the southward; they were now rapidly closing, and we made them out to be the "Felix," Sir J. Ross, with his boat towing astern, and the "Prince Albert," belonging to Lady Franklin, in charge of Commander Forsyth.

August 5th.—Plenty of water. The "Assistance" received orders to proceed (when her consort the "Intrepid" joined her) to the north shore of Lancaster Sound, examine it and Wellington Channel, and having assured themselves that Franklin had not gone up by that route to the N. W., to meet us between Cape Hotham and Cape Walker. I regretted that the shore upon which the first traces would undoubtedly be found, should have fallen to another's share: however, as there seemed a prospect of separation, and by doing so, progress, I was too rejoiced to give it a second thought; and that the "Assistance" would do her work well, was apparent to all who witnessed the zeal and skill displayed by her people in the most ordinary duty.

Taking in our ice-anchors, and getting hold of the "Resolute," I bid my friends of the "Assistance" good-bye, thinking that advance was now likely: this hope soon failed me, for again we made fast, and again we all waited for one another.

Amongst many notes of the superiority of steam over manual labour in the ice, I will extract two made to-day.

The "Assistance" was towed by the "Intrepid" in fifteen minutes, a distance which it took the "Resolute," followed by the "Pioneer," from 10 A. M. to 3 P. M. to track and warp. The "Intrepid" steamed to a berg in ten minutes, and got past it. The rest of the squadron, by manual labour, succeeded in accomplishing the same distance in three hours and a half, namely, from 7 P. M. to 10. 30 P. M., by which time the ice had closed ahead, and we had to make fast.

August 6th and 7th.—Very little progress: and a squadron of blank faces showed that there were many taking a deep and anxious interest in the state of affairs. The remark that Sir James Ross's expedition was by this time, in 1848, in a better position than ourselves, and only found time to secure winter quarters at Leopold Island, was constantly heard:

there was, in fact, but one hope left,—we had steam, and there was yet thirty days of open navigation.

Friday the 9th of August at last arrived. Captain Penny's squadron was gone out of sight in a lane of water towards Cape York. The schooner and ketch were passing us: caution yielded to the grim necessity of a push for our very honour's sake: the ship was dropped out of the nip, the "Pioneer" again allowed to put her wedge-bow, aided by steam, to the crack. In one hour we were past a barrier which had checked our advance for three long weary days. All was joy and excitement: the steamers themselves seemed to feel and know their work, and exceeded even our sanguine expectations; and, to every one's delight, we were this evening allowed to carry on a system of ice-breaking which will doubtless, in future Arctic voyages, be carried out with great success. For instance, a piece of a floe, two or three hundred yards broad, and three feet thick, prevented our progress: the weakest and narrowest part being ascertained, the ships were secured as close as possible without obstructing the steam vessels, the major part of the crews being despatched to the line where the cut was to be made, with tools and gunpowder for blasting, and plenty of short hand-lines and claws.

The "Pioneer" and "Intrepid," then, in turn rushed at the floe, breaking their way through it until the impetus gained in the open water was lost by the resistance of the ice. The word "Stop her! Back turn, easy!" was then given, and the screw went astern, carrying with her tons of ice, by means of numerous lines which the blue-jackets, who attended on the forecastle, and others on broken pieces of the floe, held on by. As the one vessel went astern, the other flew ahead to her work. The operation was, moreover, aided by the explosions of powder; and altogether the scene was a highly interesting and instructive one: it was a fresh laurel in the screw's wreath; and the gallant "Intrepid" gave a *coup-de-grace* to the mass, which sent it coach-wheeling round, as it is termed; and the whole of the squadron taking the nip, as Arctic ships should do, we were next morning in the true lead, and our troubles in Melville Bay were at an end.

It was now the 10th of August. By heavens! I shall never forget the light-heartedness of that day. Forty days had we been beset in the ice, and one day of fair application of steam, powder, and men, and the much-talked-of bay was mastered. There was, however, no time to be lost. The air was calm, the water was smooth; the land-floe (for we had again reached it) lay on the one hand—on the other the pack, from whose grip we had just escaped, still threatened us. Penny had been out of sight some time, and the "Felix" and "Prince Albert" were nearly ten miles ahead!

Gentle Reader, I'll bore you no longer! We had calm water and steam,—the ships in tow,—our progress rapid,—the "Albert" and "Felix" were caught,—their news joyfully received,—and they taken in tow likewise. The dates from England were a month later than our own: all our friends were well,—all hopeful; and, putting those last dear letters away, to be read and re-read during the coming winter, we pushed on, and there was no time to be lost. Several nights before we escaped from the pack the frost had been intense, and good sliding was to be had on the pools formed by summer heat on the floes. The bay-ice* was forming fast, and did not all melt during the day. The birds had finished breeding; and, with the fresh millions that had been added to their numbers, were feeding up preparatory to their

* First winter ice, or young ice, is called bay-ice, from an old Yorkshire word *bay*, to bend.—*Author*.

departure south. The sun was sweeping, *nightly*, nearer and nearer to the northern horizon. Night once set in, we knew full well the winter would come with giant strides. "Push on, good screw!" was on every one's lip; and anxiety was seen on every brow, if by accident, or for any purpose, the propeller ceased to move. "What's the matter? All right, I hope!" Then a chuckle of satisfaction at being told that "nothing was amiss!"

Time did not allow us, or I verily believe we might have killed tons of birds between Cape Walker and Cape York, principally little auks (*Alca alle*);—they actually blackened the edge of the floe for miles. I had seen, on the coast of Peru, near the great Guano mines, what I thought was an inconceivable number of birds congregated together; but they were as nothing compared with the myriads that we disturbed in our passage, and their stupid tameness would have enabled us to kill as many as we pleased.

On August 13th, Cape York being well in sight, Penny's brigs were again in view; and whilst the "Intrepid" and "Assistance," with the "Prince Albert," communicated with the natives of Cape York, the "Pioneer" pushed on, and soon passed the brigs, who, although they knew full well that the late arrivals from England had letters for them, were to be seen pushing tooth and nail, to get to the westward.

Slow—as slow as possible—we steamed all day along the "Crimson Cliffs of Beverley." The interview with the natives of Cape York, alas! was to cost us much. My frame of mind at the time was far from heavenly; for "Large Water" was ahead, our squadron many a long mile from its work; and I was neither interested, at the time, in Arctic Highlanders or "Crimson Snow!" In the evening the "Assistance" joined us; and I was told that "important information had been gained." We were to turn back; and the "Intrepid" went in chase of Penny, to get the aid of his interpreter, Mr. Petersen.

I remember being awoke at six o'clock on the morning of the 14th of August, and being told a hobgoblin story, which made me rub my eyes, and doubt my own hearing. What I thought of it is neither here nor there. Suffice it that Adam Beck—may he be branded for a liar!—succeeded, this day, in misleading a large number of Her Majesty's officers (as his attested document proves), and in detaining, for two days, the squadrons in search of Franklin. No one with common perception, who witnessed the interview on our deck between Mr. Petersen, Adam Beck, and our new shipmate, the Esquimaux from Cape York, could fail to perceive that Mr. P. and the Cape York native understood one another much better than the latter could the vile Adam Beck; and had I had any doubts upon the subject, they would have been removed when I learnt that Petersen had seen and communicated with these very natives before our squadron came up, and that no such bloody tale had been told him; in fact, it was the pure coinage of Adam Beck's brain, cunningly devised to keep, at any rate, his own ship on a coast whither he could escape to the neighbourhood of his home in South Greenland.

The fact of the "North Star" having wintered last year in Wolstenholme Sound, or "Petowack," was elicited, and that the natives had been on board of her. The "Assistance" and "Intrepid," therefore, remained to visit that neighbourhood, whilst we proceeded to the south shore of Lancaster Sound, touching, as had been pre-arranged, at Pond's Bay and Cape Possession.

Steaming along the Crimson Cliffs for a second time, we left the "Lady Franklin" and "Sophia," in a stark calm, to do their best. Fewer ships, the faster progress; and heartily did all cheer when, at midnight, we turned to the N. W., leaving the second division to do their work in Wolstenholme Sound. So ended the memorable 14th of August: it will be, doubtless, remembered by many with far from pleasant feelings; and some who have been "gulled" in England may thank Mr. Petersen that a carrier-pigeon freighted with a cock-and-bull story of blood, fire, wreck, and murder, was not despatched on that memorable day.

The 15th we struck westward, that is, the "Pioneer," with "Resolute" and "Prince Albert" in tow. After four hours of very intricate navigation, called "reeving through the pack," we reached the West Water,—a wide ocean of water without one piece of floe-ice, and very few icebergs. The change was wonderful—incredible. Here was nothing but water; and we were almost within sight, as we steered to the S. W., of the spot where, for forty-seven days, we had had nothing but ice! ice! ice! Let us hurry on. The West Water (as usual with the water at this season of the year) was covered with fog: in it we steered. The "Resolute," as a capital joke, in return for the long weary miles we had towed her, set, on one occasion, all studsails, and gave us a tow for four hours. When off the mouth of Lancaster Sound, the "Prince Albert" was cast off; and she departed to carry out, as I then thought, a part of the grand scheme of land travelling next year, into which it became almost daily apparent the search for Franklin would resolve itself. Already had night commenced; next came winter.

Touching at Pond's Bay was made a longer proceeding than was ever calculated upon, for a succession of thick fogs and strong gales prevented the "Pioneer" running into the bay, or ascertaining whether cairns or other marks had been erected on the coast.

The 21st of August came before we had a change of weather: happily it then took place; and the "Pioneer" (having some days before left the "Resolute," to cruise off Possession Bay) entered Pond's Bay, running up the northern shore towards a place called Button Point.

The "West Land," as this side of Baffin's Bay is called, strikes all seamen, after struggling through the icy region of Melville Bay, as being verdant and comparatively genial. We all thought so, and feasted our eyes on valleys, which, in our now humbled taste, were voted beautiful,—at any rate there were signs and symptoms of verdure; and as we steered close along the coast, green and russet colours were detected and pointed out with delight. The bay was calm and glassy, and the sun to the west, sweeping along a water horizon, showed pretty plainly that Pond's Bay, like a good many more miscalled bays of this region, was nothing more than the bell-shaped mouth to some long fiord or strait.

One of my ice-quartermasters, a highly intelligent seaman, assured me he had been in a whale-boat up this very inlet, until they conjectured themselves to be fast approaching Admiralty Inlet; the country there improved much in appearance, and in one place they found abundance of natives, deer, and grass as high as his knees. I landed with a boat's crew on Button Point. The natives had retired into the interior to kill deer and salmon: this they are in the habit of doing every season when the land ice breaks up. Numerous unroofed winter habitations and carefully secured *cachés* of seal-blubber proved that they had been here in some numbers, and would return to winter after the ice had again formed in the bay, and the seals began to appear, upon which the existence of the Esquimaux depends.

On first landing we had been startled by observing numerous cairns, standing generally in pairs: these we pulled down one after the other, and examined without finding any thing in them; and it was only the accidental discovery by one of the men of a seal-blubber *caché*, which showed that the cairns were merely marks by which the Esquimaux, on their return in the winter, could detect their stores.

The winter abode of these Esquimaux appeared to be sunk from three to four feet below the level of the ground: a ring of stones, a few feet high, were all the vestiges we saw. No doubt they completed the habitation by building a house of snow of the usual dome shape over the stones and sunken floor. Having no wood, whale-bones had been here substituted for rafters, as is usual along the whole breadth of the American coast-line from Behring's Straits; but many of the hovels had no rafters. On the whole the impression was, that the natives here lived in a state of much greater barbarity and discomfort than those we had seen about the Danish settlements on the opposite shore.

A cairn was erected by us; a record and some letters deposited for the natives to put on board whalers at a future season; and having placed a number of presents for the poor creatures in the different huts, and on the *cachés*, we hurried on board and made the best of our way to Possession Bay, and rejoined the "Resolute," from whom we learnt that the "North Star" had placed a record there, to say, that after having failed to cross Baffin's Bay in 1849, she had done so in 1850, and had gone up Lancaster Sound to seek the "Enterprise" and "Investigator," under Sir James Ross, they having, as we knew, meanwhile, gone home, been paid off, recommissioned, and were now, please God, in the Arctic Ocean, by way of Behring's Straits.

August 22d, 1850.—The "Resolute" in company, and steering a course up Lancaster Sound.

The great gateway, within whose portals we were now fast entering, has much in it that is interesting in its associations to an English seaman. Across its mouth, the bold navigator Baffin, 200 years before, had steered, pronounced it a sound, and named it after the Duke of Lancaster. About thirty-five years ago it was converted into a bay by Sir John Ross; and within eighteen months afterwards, Parry, the prince of Arctic navigators, sailed through this very bay, and discovered new lands extending half of the distance towards Behring's Straits, or about 600 miles. To complete the remaining 600 miles of unknown region, Sir John Franklin and his 140 gallant followers had devoted themselves,—with what resolution, with what devotion, is best told by their long absence and our anxiety.

The high and towering ranges of the Byam Martin Mountains looked down upon us from the southern sky, between fast-passing fog-banks and fitful gusts of wind, which soon sobbed themselves into a calm, and steam, as usual, became our friend: with it the "Pioneer," towing the "Resolute" astern, steered for the north shore of Lancaster Sound; and on August 25th we were off Croker Bay, a deep indentation between Cape Warrender and Cape Home. The clouds hung too heavily about the land, distant as we were, to see more than the bare outline, but its broken configuration gave good hope of numerous harbours, fiords, and creeks. From Cape Home, we entered on a new and peculiar region of limestone formation, lofty and tabular, offering to the seaboard cliffs steep and escarped as the imagination can picture to be possible. By the beautiful sketches of Parry's officers, made on his first voyage, we easily recognized the various headlands; the north shore being now alone in view; and indeed, except the mountains in the interior, we saw nothing more of the south shore of Lancaster Sound after leaving Possession Bay.

Of Powell Inlet we saw an extensive glacier extending into the sound, and a few loose 'berg pieces floating about. This glacier was regarded with some interest; for, remarkably enough, it is the last one met with in sailing westward to Melville Island.

The iceberg, as it is well known, is the creation of the glacier; and where land of a nature to form the latter does not exist, the former is not met with.

The region we had just left behind us is the true home of the iceberg in the northern hemisphere. There, in Baffin's Bay, where the steep cliffs of cold granitic formation frown over waters where the ordinary "deep sea lead-line" fails to find bottom, the monarch of glacial formations floats slowly from the ravine which has been its birth-place, until fairly launched in the profound waters of the Atlantic, and in the course of many years is carried to the warmer regions of the south, to assist Nature in preserving her great laws of equilibrium of temperature of the air and water.

At one period—and not a very distant one either—savans, and, amongst others, the French philosopher St. Pierre, believed icebergs to be the accumulated snow and ice of ages, which, forming at the poles, detached themselves from the parent mass: this, as they then thought, had no reference to the existence of land or water. Such an hypothesis for some time gave rise to ingenious and startling theories as to the effect which an incessant accumulation of ice would have on the globe itself; and St. Pierre hinted at the possibility of the huge cupolas of ice, which, as he believed, towered aloft in the cold heavens of the poles, suddenly launching towards the equator, melting, and bringing about a second deluge.

Had the immortal Cook been aware of the certainty of land being close to him, when, in the Antarctic regions, he found himself amongst no less than one hundred and eighty-six icebergs in December, 1773; he who, from the deck of a collier, had risen to be the Columbus of England, might have then plucked the laurel which Sir James Ross so gallantly won in the discovery of the circumpolar continent of Queen Victoria's Land.

On every side of the southern pole, on every meridian of the great South Sea, the seaman meets icebergs. Not so in the north. In the 360 degrees of longitude, which intersects the parallel of 70 degrees north (about which parallel the coasts of America, Europe, and Asia will be found to lie), icebergs are only found over an extent of some 55 degrees of longitude, and this is immediately in and about Greenland and Baffin's Bay. In fact, for 1375 miles of longitude we have icebergs, and then for 7635 geographical miles none are met with. This interesting fact is, in my opinion, most cheering, and points strongly to the possibility that no extensive land exists about our northern pole,—a supposition which is borne out by the fact, that the vast ice-fields off Spitzbergen show no symptoms of ever having been in contact with land or gravel. Of course, the more firmly we can bring ourselves to believe in the existence of an ocean road leading to Behring's Straits, the better heart we shall feel in searching the various tortuous channels and different islands with which, doubtless, Franklin's route has been beset. It was not, therefore, without deep interest that I passed the boundary which Nature had set in the west to the existence of icebergs, and endeavoured to form a correct idea of the cause of such a phenomenon.

Whilst this digression upon icebergs has taken place, the kind reader will suppose the calm to have ceased, and the

"Resolute" and "Pioneer," under sail before a westerly wind, to be running from the table-land on the north shore of Lancaster Sound, in a diagonal direction towards Leopold Island. On the 26th of August, Cape York gleamed through an angry sky, and as Regent's Inlet opened to the southward, there was little doubt but we should soon be caught in an Arctic gale: we, however, cared little, provided there was plenty of water ahead, though of that there appeared strong reasons for entertaining doubts, as both the temperature of the air and water was fast falling.

That night—for night was now of some two hours' duration—the wind piped merrily, and we rolled most cruelly; the long and narrow "Pioneer" threatening to pitch every spar over the side, and refusing all the manœuvring upon the part of her beshaken officers and men to comfort and quiet her.

A poet, who had not been fourteen hours in the cold, and whose body was not racked by constant gymnastic exertion to preserve his bones from fracture, might have given a beautiful description of the lifting of a fierce sky at about half-past one in the morning, and a disagreeable glimpse through snow-storm and squall of a bold and precipitous coast not many miles off, and ahead of us. I cannot undertake to do so, for I remember feeling far from poetical, as, with a jerk and a roll, the "Pioneer," under fore and aft canvas, came to the wind. Fast increasing daylight showed us to have been thrown considerably to the northward; and as we sailed to the south the ice showed itself in far from pleasing proximity under the lee—*boiling*, for so the edge of a pack appears to do in a gale of wind. It was a wild sight; but we felt that, at any rate, it was optional with a screw steamer whether she ran into the pack or kept the sea, for her clawing-to-windward power astonished us who had fought in the teeth of hard gales elsewhere in flying Symondite brigs. Not so, however, thought a tough old Hull quartermaster, whose weather-beaten face peered anxiously over the lee, and watched the "Resolute" beating Cromer-a-lee, for I heard him growl out, "Wull, if they are off a strait lee-pack edge, the sooner they make up their minds to run into it the better!" "Why so, Hall?" I inquired. "Because, sir," replied the old man, "that ship is going two feet to leeward for one she is going ahead, and she would *never* work off *nothing!*"

"Pleasant!" I mentally ejaculated; but, willing to hear more from my dry old friend, who was quite a character in his way,—"Perhaps," I said, "you have occasionally been caught in worse vessels off such a pack as you describe, or a lee shore, and still not been lost?"

"Oh! Lord, sir! we have some rum craft in the whaling ships, but I don't think any thing so sluggish as the 'Resolute.' Howsomdever, they gets put to it now and then. Why, it was only last year, we were down on the south-west fishing-ground: about the 10th of October, it came on to blow, sir, from the southward, and sent in a sea upon us, which nearly drowned us: we tried to keep an offing, but it was no use; we couldn't show a rag; every thing was blown away, and it was perishing cold; but our captain was a smart man, and he said,—'Well, boys, we must run for Hangman's Cove,* altho' it's late in the day; if we don't, I won't answer where we'll be in the morning."

"So up we put the helm, sir, to run for a place like a hole in a wall, with nothing but a close-reefed topsail set, and the sky as thick as pea-soup. It looked a bad job, I do assure

* Hangman's Cove, a small harbour on the west side of Davis's Straits.

you, sir. Just as it was dark, we found ourselves right up against the cliffs, and we did not know whether we were lost or saved until by good luck we shot into dead smooth water in a little cove, and let go our anchor. Next day a calm set in, and the young ice made round the ship: we couldn't cut it, and we couldn't tow the vessel through it. We had not three months' provisions, and we made certain sure of being starved to death; when the wind came strong off the land, and, by working for our lives, we escaped, and went home directly out of the country."

"A cheering tale, this, of the Hangman's Cove," I thought, as I turned from my Job's comforter; and, satisfying myself that the pack precluded all chance of reaching Leopold Island for the present, I retired to rest.

Next day, the 27th of August, found us steering past Cape Hurd, off which the pack lay at a distance of some ten miles, and, as we ran westward, and the breadth of clear water gradually diminished, the wind failed us; although, astern in Lancaster Sound, there was still a dark and angry sky betokening a war of the elements, whereas where we were off Radstock Bay—all was calm, cold, and arctic.

"Up steam, and take in tow!" was again the cry; and as the pack, acted on by the tide, commenced to travel quickly in upon Cape Ricketts, we slipped past it, and reached an elbow formed between that headland and Beechey Island. The peculiar patch of broken table-land, called Caswell's Tower, as well as the striking cliffs of slaty limestone along whose base we were rapidly steaming, claimed much of our attention; and we were pained to see, from the strong ice-blink to the S. W., that a body of packed ice had been driven up the straits by the late gales.

The sun was fast dipping behind North Devon, and a beautiful moon (the first we had found any use for since passing Cape Farewell on the 28th of May) was cheerfully accepted as a substitute, when the report of a boat being seen from the mast-head startled us and excited general anxiety. We were then off Gascoigne Inlet, the "Resolute" in tow. The boat proved to be the "Sophia's," and in her Captain Stewart and Dr. Sutherland; they went on board the "Resolute," and, shortly afterwards, the interesting intelligence they then communicated was made known to me.

It was this,—the "Assistance" and "Intrepid," after they left us, had visited Wolstenholme Sound, and discovered the winter quarters of H. M. S. "North Star," but nothing to lead them to place any faith in Adam Beck's tale: from thence they had examined the north shore of Lancaster Sound as far as Cape Riley, without discovering any thing; on landing there, however, numerous traces of English seamen having visited the spot were discovered in sundry pieces of rag, rope, broken bottles, and a long-handled instrument intended to rake up things from the bottom of the sea; marks of a tent-place were likewise visible. A cairn was next seen on Beechey Island; to this the "Intrepid" proceeded, and, as rather an odd incident connected with her search of this spot took place, I shall here mention it, although it was not until afterwards that the circumstance came to my knowledge.

The steamer having approached close under the island, a boat-full of officers and men proceeded on shore: on landing, some relics of European visitors were found; and we can picture the anxiety with which the steep was scaled and the cairn torn down, every stone turned over, the ground underneath dug up a little, and yet, alas! no document or record found. Meanwhile an Arctic adventure, natural, but novel to one portion of the actors, was taking place. The boat had left the "Intrepid" without arms of any description, and the people on the top of the cliff saw, to their dismay, a large white bear advancing rapidly in the direction of the boat, which, by the deliberate way the brute stopped and raised his head as if in the act of smelling, appeared to disturb his olfactory nerves. The two men left in charge of the boat happily caught sight of Bruin before he caught hold of them, and launching the boat they hurried off to the steamer, whilst the observers left on the cliff were not sorry to see the bear chase the boat a short way and then turn towards the packed ice in the offing. This event, together with some risk of the ice separating the two vessels, induced the party to return on board, where a general (though, as was afterwards proved, erroneous) impression had been created on the minds of the people belonging to the two ships, that what they had found must be the traces of a retreating or shipwrecked party from the "Erebus" and "Terror." A short distance within Cape Riley, another tent-place was found; and then, after a look at the coast up as far as Cape Innis, the two vessels proceeded across towards Cape Hotham, on the opposite side of Wellington Channel, having in the first place erected a cairn at the base of Cape Riley, and in it deposited a document.

Whilst the "Assistance" and "Intrepid" were so employed, the American squadron, and that under Captain Penny, were fast approaching. The Americans first communicated with Captain Ommanney's division, and heard of the discovery of the first traces of Sir John Franklin. The Americans then informed Penny, who was pushing for Wellington Channel; and he, after some trouble, succeeded in catching the "Assistance," and, on going on board of her, learnt all they had to tell him, and saw what traces they had discovered. Captain Penny then returned—as he figuratively expressed it—"to take up the search from Cape Riley like a blood-hound," and richly was he rewarded for doing so.

At Cape Spencer he discovered the ground-plan of a tent, the floor of which was neatly and carefully paved with small smooth stones. Around the tent a number of bird's bones, as well as remnants of meat-canisters, led him to imagine that it had been inhabited for some time as a shooting station and a look-out place, for which latter purpose it was admirably chosen, commanding a good view of Barrow's Strait and Wellington Channel; this opinion was confirmed by the discovery of a piece of paper, on which was written, "to be called,"—evidently the fragments of an officer's night orders.

Some sledge marks pointed northward from this neighbourhood; and, the American squadron being unable to advance up the strait (in consequence of the ice resting firmly against the land close to Cape Innis, and across to Barlow Inlet on the opposite shore), Lieut. de Haven despatched parties on foot to follow these sledge marks, whilst Penny's squadron returned to re-examine Beechey Island. The American officers found the sledge tracts very distinct for some miles, but before they had got as far as Cape Bowden, the trail ceased, and one empty bottle and a piece of newspaper were the last things found in that direction.

Not so Captain Penny's squadron:—making fast to the ice between Beechey Island and Cape Spencer, in what is now called Union Bay, and in which they found the "Felix" schooner to be likewise lying, parties from the "Lady Franklin" and "Sophia" started towards Beechey Island.

A long point of land slopes gradually from the southern bluffs of this now deeply interesting island, until it almost connects itself with the land of North Devon, forming, on either side of it, two good and commodious bays. On this slope, a multitude of preserved meat-tins were strewed about, and near them, and on the ridge of the slope, a carefully constructed cairn was discovered: it consisted of layers of meat-tins filled with gravel, and placed to form a solid foundation. Beyond this, and along the northern shore of Beechey Island, the following traces were then quickly discovered:—the embankment of a house with carpenter and armourer's working-places, washing-tubs, coal-bags, pieces of old clothing, rope, and, lastly, the graves of three of the crew of the "Erebus" and "Terror,"—placing it beyond all doubt, that the missing ships had indeed been there, and bearing date of the winter of 1845–46.

We, therefore, now had ascertained the first winter quarters of Sir John Franklin! Here fell to the ground all the evil forebodings of those who had, in England, consigned his expedition to the depths of Baffin's Bay, on its outward voyage. Our first prayer had been granted by a beneficent Providence; and we had now risen, from doubt and hope, to a certain assurance of Franklin having reached thus far without shipwreck or disaster.

Leaving us in high spirits at the receipt of such glorious intelligence, Captain Stewart proceeded in his boat to search the coast-line towards Gascoigne Inlet and Caswell's Tower. We continued to steam on; off Cape Riley a boat was despatched to examine the record left by the "Assistance;" and, from her, I heard that the "Prince Albert," which had been ordered by Lady Franklin down Regent's Inlet to Brentford Bay, had visited the said cairn, deposited a document to say so, and was gone, I now felt certain, home.

As the "Pioneer" slowly steamed through the loose ice which lay off Beechey Island, the cairn erected by Franklin's people on the height above us was an object of deep interest and conversation; and, placed so conspicuously as it was, it seemed to say to the beating heart, "Follow them that erected me!"

On rounding the western point, three brigs and a schooner were seen to be fast to the land ice in Union Bay; and, as we had been in the habit of almost scraping the cliffs in Baffin's Bay, I, forgetting the difference between the approach to a granite and a limestone cliff, and desirous to avoid the stream of ice now pouring out of Wellington Channel, went too close to the shore, and eventually ran aground; the "Resolute" just saved herself by slipping the tow-rope, and letting go an anchor. A rapidly-falling tide soon showed me that I must be patient and wait until next day, and, as the "Resolute" was in the course of the night worked into the bay, and sécured, we "piped down" for awhile.

Wednesday, 28th August.—I was awoke by a hearty shake, and Captain Penny's warm "Good-morning;" he had come out to me towing the "Mary," a launch belonging to Sir John Ross, in order that I might lighten the "Pioneer," and offered me the "Sophia" brig, to receive a portion of my stores, if I would only say it was necessary.

"A friend in need is a friend indeed," and such Captain Penny proved himself; for my position was far from a pleasant one,—on a hard spit of limestone, in which no anchor could find holding ground, and, at low water, five feet less than the draught of the "Pioneer," exposed to all the set of the ice of the Wellington Channel and Barrow's Strait, with about another week of the "open season" left.

All arrangements having been made to try and float the steamer at high water, I had time to ask Captain Penny his news; the best part of which was, that as yet nothing had been found in our neighbourhood to lead to the inference that any party in distress had retreated from the "Erebus" and "Terror." He considered the harbour chosen by Franklin for his winter quarters was an excellent one.

Captain Penny gave no very cheering account of the prospect of a much farther advance for ourselves: Wellington Channel was blocked up with a very heavy floe, and Barrow's Strait to the westward was choked with packed ice; the "Assistance" and "Intrepid" were to be seen off Barlow Inlet, but their position was far from a secure one; and, lastly, Penny told me he intended, after the result of a fresh search for a record on Beechey Island was known, to communicate with the "Assistance," in order that Captain Ommanney might be fully informed of all that had been discovered, and that we might learn whether any thing had been found at Cape Hotham.

On the 29th of August, the "Pioneer," much to my joy, was again afloat, and fast to the ice in company with the other vessels; and, although my officers and crew were well fagged out with forty-eight hours' hard labour, parties of them, myself amongst the number, were to be seen trudging across the ice of Union Bay towards Franklin's winter quarters.

It needed not a dark wintry sky nor a gloomy day to throw a sombre shade around my feelings as I landed on Beechey Island and looked down upon the bay, on whose bosom once had ridden Her Majesty's ships "Erebus" and "Terror;" there was a sickening anxiety of the heart as one involuntarily clutched at every relic they of Franklin's squadron had left behind, in the vain hope that some clue as to the route they had taken hence might be found.

From the cairn to the long and curving beach, from the frozen surface of the bay to the tops of the distant cliffs, the eye involuntarily but keenly sought for something more than had yet been found.

But, no; as sharp eyes, as anxious hearts, had already been there, and I was obliged to be content with the information, which my observation proved to be true, that the search had been close and careful, but that nothing was to be found in the shape of written record.

On the eastern slope of the ridge of Beechey Island, a remnant of a garden (for remnant it now only was, having been dug up in the search) told an interesting tale: its neatly-shaped oval outline, the border carefully formed of moss, lichen, poppies, and anemones, transplanted from some more genial part of this dreary region, contrived still to show symptoms of vitality; but the seeds which doubtless they had sown in the garden had decayed away. A few hundred yards lower down, a mound, the foundation of a storehouse, was next to be seen; the ground-plan was somewhat thus:—

North side, 61½ feet long.

A B. B D. } Exterior embankments, about four feet through at the base and five feet
A C. E F. } high, in which posts had been sunk.

K L. An interior embankment of same description enclosing a space, supposed store; had marks of posts in it likewise.

C E. and F D. The doorways.

H. Evidently a carpenter's workshop, from the shavings, &c.

It consisted of an exterior and interior embankment, into which, from the remnants left, we saw that oak and elm scantling had been struck as props to the roofing; in one part of the enclosed space some coal-sacks were found, and in another part numerous wood-shavings proved the ship's artificers to have been working here. The generally received opinion as to the object of this storehouse was, that Franklin had constructed it to shelter a portion of his superabundant provisions and stores, with which it was well known his decks were lumbered on leaving Whale-Fish Islands.

Nearer to the beach, a heap of cinders and scraps of iron showed the armourer's working-place; and along an old water-course, now chained up by frost, several tubs, constructed of the ends of salt-meat casks, left no doubt as to the washing-places of the men of Franklin's squadron: happening to cross a level piece of ground, which as yet no one had lighted upon, I was pleased to see a pair of Cashmere gloves laid out to dry, with two small stones on the palms to prevent their blowing away; they had been there since 1846. I took them up carefully, as melancholy mementoes of my missing friends. In another spot a flannel was discovered: and this, together with some things lying about, would, in my ignorance of wintering in the Arctic Regions, have led me to suppose that there was considerable haste displayed in the departure of the "Erebus" and "Terror" from this spot, had not Captain Austin assured me that there was nothing to ground such a belief upon; and that, from experience, he could vouch for these being nothing more than the ordinary traces of a winter station, and this opinion was fully borne out by those officers who had in the previous year wintered at Port Leopold, one of them asserting that people left winter quarters too well pleased to escape to care much for a handful of shavings, an old coal-bag, or a washing-tub. This I from experience now know to be true.

Looking at the spot on which Penny had discovered a boarding-pike, and comparing it with a projecting point on the opposite side, where a similar article had been found with a finger nailed on it as a direction-post, I concluded that, in a line between these two boarding-pikes, one or both of the ships had been at anchor, and this conjecture was much borne out by the relative positions of the other traces found; and besides this, a small cairn on the crest of Beechey Island appears to have been intended as a meridian mark, and, if so, Franklin's squadron undoubtedly lay where I would place it, far and effectually removed from all risk of being swept out of the bay, which, by the bye, from the fact of the enclosed area being many times broader than the entrance of "Erebus and Terror Bay," was about as probable as any stout gentleman being blown out of a house through the keyhole. In the one case the stout individual would have to be cut up small, in the other case the ice would have to be well broken up; and if so, it was not likely Franklin would allow himself to be taken out of harbour, *nolens volens*, whilst he had anchors to hook the ground with, and ice-saws, with which his crews could have cut through *a mile of ice three feet thick in twenty-four hours.*

The graves next attracted our attention; they, like all that English seamen construct, were scrupulously neat. Go where you will over the globe's surface, afar in the East, or afar in the West, down amongst the coral-girded isles of the South Sea, or here where the grim North frowns on the sailor's grave, you will always find it alike; it is the monument raised by rough hands, but affectionate hearts, over the last home of their messmate; it breathes of the quiet churchyard in some of England's many nooks, where each had formed his idea of what was due to departed worth; and the ornaments that Nature decks herself with, even in the desolation of the Frozen Zone, were carefully culled to mark the dead seamen's home. The good taste of the officers had prevented the general simplicity of an oaken head and foot-board to each of the three graves being marred by any long and childish epitaphs, or the doggerel of a lower-deck poet, and the three inscriptions were as follows:—

"Sacred to the memory of J. Torrington, who departed this life, January 1st, 1846, on board of H. M. S. 'Terror,' aged 20 years."

"Sacred to the memory of Wm. Braine, R. M., of H. M. S. 'Erebus;' died April 3d, 1846, aged 32 years.

"'Choose ye this day whom ye will serve.'—Josh. xxiv. 15."

"Sacred to the memory of J. Hartwell, A. B., of H. M. S. 'Erebus;' died January 4th, 1846, aged 25 years.

"'Thus saith the Lord of Hosts, consider your ways.'—Haggai i. 7."

I thought I traced in the epitaphs over the graves of the men from the "Erebus," the manly and Christian spirit of Franklin. In the true spirit of chivalry, he, their captain and leader, led them amidst dangers and unknown difficulties with iron will stamped upon his brow, but the words of meekness, gentleness, and truth, were his device. We have seen his career and we know his deeds!

> "Why should their praise in verse be sung?
> The name that dwells on every tongue
> No minstrel needs."

From the graves, a tedious ascent up the long northern slope of Beechey Island carried us to the table-land, on whose southern verge, a cairn of stones, to which I have before referred, was placed; it had been several times pulled down by different searchers, and dug up underneath, but carefully replaced. The position was an admirable one, and appeared as if intentionally chosen to attract the attention of vessels coming up Barrow's Strait: from it, on the day I was up, the view was so extensive, that, did I not feel certain of being supported by all those who have, like myself, witnessed the peculiar clearness, combined with refraction, of the atmosphere in Polar climes, I should bear in mind the French adage,—"La verité n'est pas toujours le vraisemblable," and hold my peace.

To the west, the land of Cornwallis Island stretched up Wellington Channel for many miles, and Cape Hotham locked with Griffith's Island. In the south-west a dark mass of land showed Cape Walker, and from Cape Bunny, the southern shore of Barrow's Strait spread itself until terminated in the steep wall-like cliffs of Cape Clarence and Leopold Island.

This latter spot, so interesting from having been the winter quarters of the late relieving squadron under Sir James Ross, looked ridiculously close,—to use a seaman's term, it appeared as if a biscuit might have been tossed upon it; and the thought involuntarily rose to one's mind,—Would to God that, in 1848, Sir James Ross had known that within forty miles of him Franklin had wintered.

I have now nearly enumerated all the important points, to which, at all hours of the day and night, parties from the eight vessels assembled in Union Bay were constantly wending their way and returning; but around the whole island there were abundant proofs of the missing expedition having been no sluggards; for there was hardly a foot of the beach-line which did not show signs of their having been there before us, either in shooting excursions or other pursuits, and usually in the shape of a preserved-meat tin, a piece of rope, or a strip of canvas or rag.

On the eastern extreme of Beechey Island, and under a beetling cliff which formed the entrance to the bay, a very neatly-paved piece of ground denoted a tent-place; much pains had been bestowed upon it, and a pigmy terrace had been formed around their abode, the margin of which was decorated with moss and poppy plants: in an adjacent gully a shooting-gallery had been established, as appeared by the stones placed at proper distances, and a large tin marked "Soup and Bouilli," which, perforated with balls, had served for a target. I carefully scanned the flat slabs of slaty limestone, of which the over-hanging cliffs were formed, in hopes of seeing some name, or date, scratched upon the surface; some clue, mayhap, to the information we so dearly longed for,—the route taken by Franklin on sailing hence, whether to Cape Walker or up Wellington Channel. But, no; the silent cliff bore no mark; by some fatality, the proverbial love for marking their names, or telling their tales, on every object, which I have ever found in seamen, was here an exception, and I turned to my vessel, after three unprofitable walks on Beechey Island, with the sad conviction on my mind, that, instead of being able to concentrate the wonderful resources we had now at hand about Beechey Island in one line of search, we should be obliged to take up the three routes which it was probable Franklin might have taken in 1846; viz., S. W. by Cape Walker, N. W. by Wellington Channel, or W. by Melville Island,—a division of force tending to weaken the chance of reaching Franklin as quickly as we could wish, unless circumstances were peculiarly favourable.

Vague reports of some of Captain Penny's people having seen sledge-marks on the eastern shores of "Erebus and Terror

Bay," induced one of the officers of the "Pioneer" and myself to arrange with Captain Penny to take a walk in that direction.

Landing on the north shore of Union Bay, at the base of the cliffs of Cape Spencer, we were soon pointed out a deep sledge-mark, which had cut through the edge of one of the ancient tide-marks, or terraces, and pointed in a direct line from the cairn of meat-tins erected by Franklin, on the northern spur of Beechey Island, to a valley which led towards the bay between Capes Innis and Bowden. I conceived the trail to be that of an outward-bound sledge, on account of its depth, which denoted a heavily-ladened one.

Proceeding onward, our party were all much struck with the extraordinary regularity of the terraces, which, with almost artificial parallelism, swept round the base of the limestone cliffs and hills of North Devon. That they were ancient tidal-marks, now raised to a considerable elevation above the sea by the upheaval of the land, I was the more inclined to believe, from the numerous fossil shells, crustacea, and corallines which strewed the ground. The latter witnesses to a once more genial condition of climate in these now inclement regions, carried us back to the sun-blest climes, where the blue Pacific lashes the coral-guarded isles of sweet Otaheite, and I must plead guilty to a recreant sigh for past recollections and dear friends, all summoned up by the contemplation of a fragment of fossil-coral.

The steep abutment of the cliffs on the north of "Erebus and Terror Bay," obliged us to descend to the floe, along the surface of which we rapidly progressed, passing the point on which the pike used by Franklin's people as a direction-post had been found. At a point where these said cliffs receded to the N. E., and towards the head of Gascoigne Inlet, leaving a long strip of low land, which, connecting itself with the bluffs of Cape Riley, forms the division between Gascoigne Inlet and "Erebus and Terror Bay," a perfect congery of sledge-marks showed the spot used for the landing-place, or rendezvous, of Franklin's sledges.

Some of these sledge-marks swept towards Cape Riley, doubtless towards the traces found by the "Assistance;" others, and those of heavily-ladened sledges, ran northward, into a gorge through the hills, whilst the remainder pointed towards Caswell's Tower, a remarkable mass of limestone, which, isolated at the bottom of Radstock Bay, forms a conspicuous object to a vessel approaching this neighbourhood from the eastward or westward.

Deciding to follow the latter trail, we separated the party in such a manner, that, if one lost the sledge-marks, others would pick them up.

Arriving at the margin of a lake, which was only one of a series, and tasted decidedly brackish, though its connection with the sea was not apparent, we found the site of a circular tent, unquestionably that of a shooting-party from the "Erebus" or "Terror." The stones used for keeping down the canvas lay around; three or four large ones, well blackened by smoke, had been the fire-place; a porter-bottle or two, several meat-tins, pieces of paper, birds' feathers, and scraps of the fur of Arctic hares, were strewed about. Eagerly did we run from one object to the other, in the hope of finding some stray note or record, to say whether all had been well with them, and whither they had gone. No, not a line was to be found. Disappointed, but not beaten, we turned to follow up the trail.

The sledge-marks consisted of two parallel lines, about two feet apart, and sometimes three or four inches deep into the gravel, or broken limestone, of which the whole plain seemed to be formed. The difficulty of dragging a sledge over such ground, and under such circumstances, must have been great, and, between the choice of evils, the sledge-parties appeared at last to have preferred taking to the slope of the hills, as being easier travelling than the stony plain. A fast-rising gale, immediately in our faces, with thick, driving snow and drift, suddenly obscured the land about us, and rendered our progress difficult and hazardous.

After edging to the northward for some time, as if to strike the head of Gascoigne Inlet, the trail struck suddenly down upon the plain: we did the same, and as suddenly lost our clue, though there was no doubt on any of our minds, but that the sledge had gone towards Caswell's Tower; for us to go there was, however, now impossible, having no compass, and the snow-storm preventing us seeing more than a few hundred yards ahead. We therefore turned back walking across the higher grounds direct for the head of Union Bay, a route which gave us considerable insight into the ravine-rent condition of this limestone country, at much cost of bodily fatigue to ourselves. The glaciers in the valleys, or ravines, hardly deserved the name, after the monsters we had seen in Baffin's Bay, and, I should think, in extraordinary seasons, they often melted away altogether, for, in spite of so severe a one as the present year had been, there was but little ice remaining.

The gale raged fiercely as the day drew on, and, on getting sight of Wellington Channel, the wild havoc amongst the ice made us talk anxiously of that portion of our squadron which was now on the opposite or lee side of the channel, as well as the American squadron that had pushed up to the edge of the fixed ice beyond Point Innis.

Seven hours' hard walking left us pretty well done up by the time we tumbled into our boat, and, thanks to the stalwart strokes of Captain Stewart's oar, we soon reached the

"Pioneer," and enjoyed our dinner with more than the usually keen appetite of Arctic seamen.

Such were the traces found in and about Franklin's winter quarters: one good result had arisen from their discovery,—the safe passage of Franklin across the dangers of Baffin's Bay was no longer a question; this was a certainty, and it only remained for us to ascertain which route he had taken, and then to follow him.

Wellington Channel engrossed much attention; the Americans, with true go-ahead spirit, watched the ice in it most keenly. The gallant commander of their expedition, De Haven, had already more than once pushed his craft up an angle of water north of Point Innis; his second, Mr. Griffin, in the "Rescue," was hard at work obtaining angles, by which to ascertain the fact of Wellington Channel being a channel or a fiord, a point as yet undecided, for there was a break in the land to the N. W. which left the question still at issue.

Captain Penny, with his vessels, got under weigh one day, and ran over towards the "Assistance," as far as the pack would allow him, and then despatched an officer with a boat to communicate our intelligence as well as his own; a sudden change of weather obliged Penny to return, and the boat's crew of the "Lady Franklin," on their way back, under Mr. John Stuart, underwent no small risk and labour. They left the "Assistance" to walk to their boat, which had been hauled on the ice; a thick fog came on; the direction was with difficulty maintained; no less than eleven bears were seen prowling around the party; the boat was found by mere accident, and, after fourteen hours' incessant walking and pulling, Mr. Stuart succeeded in reaching the "Lady Franklin."

Through him we learnt that Cape Hotham and the neighbourhood of Barlow Inlet showed no sign of having been visited by Franklin, that the pack was close home against the land, and that the "Assistance" and "Intrepid" had been subject to some pressure, but were all safe and sound.

Almost every hour during our detention in Union Bay, large flights of wild fowl, principally geese and eider ducks, flew past us, as if they had come down Wellington Channel, and were making away to the southward; this certain indication of approaching winter was not to be mistaken, and we anxiously counted the hours which kept flitting past, whilst we were chained up in Union Bay.

South-easterly winds forced the pack tighter and tighter in Wellington Channel, and once or twice it threatened to beset us even in Union Bay; and on the 31st of August our position was still the same, the Americans being a little in advance, off Point Innis.

From the 1st to the 4th of September, we lay wishing for an opening, the Americans working gallantly along the edge of the fixed ice of Wellington Channel, towards Barlow Inlet.

September the 5th brought the wished-for change. A lead of water. Hurrah! up steam! take in tow! every one's spirits up to the high-top-gallant of their joy; long streaks of water showing across Wellington Channel, out of which broad floe-pieces were slowly sailing, whilst a hard, cold appearance in the northern sky betokened a northerly breeze.

With the "Resolute" fast astern, the "Pioneer" slipped round an extensive field of ice; as it ran aground off Cape Spencer, shutting off in our rear Captain Penny's brigs and the "Felix," another mass of ice at the same time caught on Point Innis, and, unable to get past it, we again made fast, sending a boat to watch the moment the ice should float, and leave us a passage to the westward. Whilst thus secured, we had abundant amusement and occupation in observing the movements of shoals of white whales. They were what the fishermen on board called "running" south, a term used to express the steady and rapid passage of the fish from one feeding-ground to the other. From the mast-head, the water about us appeared filled with them, whilst they constantly rose and blew, and hurried on, like the birds we had lately seen, to better regions in the south. That they had been north to breed was undoubted, by the number of young "calves" in every shoal. The affection between mother and young was very evident; for occasionally some stately white whale would loiter on her course, as if to scrutinize the new and strange objects now floating in these unploughed waters, whilst the calf, all gambols, rubbed against the mother's side, or played about her. The proverbial shyness of these fish was proved by our fishermen and sportsmen to be an undoubted fact, for neither with harpoon nor rifle-ball could they succeed in capturing any of them.

It was a subject of deep interest and wonder to see this migration of animal life, and I determined, directly leisure would enable me, to search the numerous books with which we were well stored, to endeavour to satisfy my mind with some reasonable theory, founded upon the movements of bird and fish, as to the existence of a Polar ocean or a Polar continent.

A sudden turn of tide, which floated the ice that had for some hours been aground on Point Innis and Cape Spencer, and carried it out of Wellington Channel, which favourable tide I therefore conjectured to be the flood, enabled the "Pioneer" and "Resolute" to start across Wellington Channel, towards Barlow Inlet.

Northward of us, ran, almost in a straight line, east and west, the southern edge of a body of ice, which we then imagined, in our ignorance, to be *fixed*, extending northward,

—aye, to the very pole; for in the rumour of it being a mere fiord, or gulf, I had no belief, nor any one else who crossed it in our ships. The day was beautifully clear, and a cold, hard sky enabled us to see the land of North Somerset most distinctly, though thirty to forty miles distant; and yet nothing appeared resembling land in the northern part of Wellington Channel. More than one of us regretted the prospect of this yet unsearched route remaining so, and the racing mania for Melville Island and Cape Walker bore for all of us this day its fruit—unavailing regret.

A fresh and favourable gale from the northward raised our spirits and hopes, late as it now was in the season, and already, with the adventurous feelings of seamen, we began to calculate what distance might yet be achieved, should the breeze but last for two or three days. The space to be traversed, even to Behring's Straits, was a mere nothing; and all our disappointments, all our foiled anticipations, were forgotten, in the light-heartedness brought about by a day of open water and a few hours of a fair wind. As we rattled along the lane of blue water which wound gracefully ahead to the westward, the shores of Cornwallis Island rapidly revealed themselves, and offered little that was striking or picturesque. One uniform tint of russet-brown clothed the land, as the sun at eight in the evening sunk behind the ice-bound horizon of Wellington Channel.

Novel and striking as were the colours thrown athwart the cold, hard sky by the setting orb, I thought with a sigh of those gay and flickering shades which beautify the heavens in the tropics, when the fierce sun sinks to his western rest. No gleams of purple and gold lit up the hill-tops; no fiery streaks of sunlight streamed across the water, or glittered on the wave. No! all was cold and silent as the grave. In heaven alone there appeared sunshine and vitality:—it was rightly so. Frost was fast claiming its dominion, for, with declining sunlight, the space of water between the pack and the floe became a sheet of young ice, about the one-eighth of an inch in thickness.

The "Assistance" and "Intrepid" were gone, it was very evident; but the American squadron was observed in Barlow Inlet. As we approached them, at two o'clock in the morning, they were to be seen firing muskets. We therefore put our helms down, and performed, by the help of the screw, figures of eight in the young ice, until a boat had communicated with Commander De Haven, from whom we learned that one of his vessels was aground in the inlet, and that it was no place for us to go into, unless we wanted to remain there. The passage to the westward, round Cape Hotham, was likewise blocked up, and no alternative remained but to make fast to the floe to the north of us. This was done, and just in time; for a smart breeze from the S. E. brought up a great deal of ice, and progress in any direction was impossible.

I had now time to observe that the floe of Wellington Channel, instead of consisting of a mass of ice (as was currently reported) about eight feet in thickness, did not in average depth exceed that of the floes of Melville Bay, although a great deal of old ice was mixed up with it, as if a pack had been re-cemented by a winter's frost; in which case, of course, there would be ice of various ages mixed up in the body; and much of the ice was lying crosswise and edgeways, so that a person desirous of looking at the Wellington Channel floe, as the accumulation of many years of continued frost, might have some grounds upon which to base his supposition. A year's observation, however, has shown me the fallacy of supposing that in deep-water channels floes continue to increase in thickness from year to year; and to that subject I will return in a future chapter, when treating of Wellington Channel.

The closing chapter of accidents, by which the navigation of 1850 was brought to a close by the squadrons in search of Sir John Franklin, is soon told.

The "Resolute" and "Pioneer" remained, unable to move, in Wellington Channel; a northerly gale came on, after a short breeze from the S. E.; and imagine, kind reader, our dismay, in finding the vast expanse, over which the eye had in vain strained to see its limit—imagine this field suddenly breaking itself across in all directions, from some unseen cause, farther than (as appeared to us) a northerly gale blowing over its surface, and our poor barks, in its cruel embrace, sweeping out of Wellington Channel, and then towards Leopold Island. At one time, the probability of reaching the Atlantic, as Sir James Ross did, stared us disagreeably in the face, and blank indeed did we all look at such a prospect.

A calm and frosty morning ushered in the 9th of September. The pack was fast re-knitting itself, and we were drifting with it, one mile per hour, to the S. E., when Penny's brigs, that had been seen the day before crossing to the northward of us, were observed to be running down along the western shore, with the American squadron ahead of them, the latter having just escaped from an imprisonment in Barlow Inlet. About the same time, a temporary opening of the pack enabled the steam-power again to be brought to bear, and never was it more useful. The pack was too small and broken for a vessel to warp or heave through, there was no wind "to bore" through it, and the young ice in some places, by pressure, was nigh upon six inches thick; towing with boats was, therefore, out of the question.

The "Resolute" fast astern, with a long scope of hawser,

the "Pioneer," like a prize-fighter, settled to her work, and went in and won. The struggle was a hard one,—now through sludge and young ice, which gradually checked her headway, impeded as she was with a huge vessel astern—now in a strip of open water, mending her pace to rush at a bar of broken-up pack, which surged and sailed away as her fine bow forced through it—now cautiously approaching a nip between two heavy floe pieces, which time and the screw wedged slowly apart—and then the subdued cheer with which our crews witnessed all obstacles overcome, and the Naval expedition again in open water, and close ahead of the Government one under Penny, and Commander De Haven's gallant vessels, who, under a press of canvas, were just hauling round Cape Hotham. A light air and bay-ice gave us every advantage.

Next day, in succession, we all came up to the "Assistance" and "Intrepid," fast at a floe edge, between Cape Bunny and Griffith's Island. That this floe was not a fixed one we were assured, as the "Intrepid" had been between it and Griffith's Island, nearly as far as Somerville Island; but, unhappily, it barred our road as effectually as if it were so. Penny, with his squadron, failed in passing southward towards Cape Walker; and Lieutenant Cator, in the "Intrepid" was equally unsuccessful.

I was much interested in the account of the gallant struggle of the "Assistance" and "Intrepid" in rounding Cape Hotham. They fairly fought their way against the ice, which at every east-going tide was sweeping out of Barrow's Strait, and grinding along the shore. It is most satisfactory to see that all risks may be run, and yet neither ships nor crews be lost; and it is but fair to suppose, that, if our ships incurred such dangers unscathed, the "sweet cherub" will not a jot the less have watched over the "Erebus" and "Terror."

Of course, the "croakers" say, if the floe had pressed a *little* more—if the ship had risen a *little* less—in fact, if Providence had been a *little* less watchful—disasters must have overtaken our ships; but when I hear these "dismal Jemmies" croak, it puts me much in mind of the midshipman, who, describing to his grandmamma the attack on Jean d'Acre, after recounting his prowess and narrow escapes, assured the old lady that Tom Tough, the boatswain's mate, had asserted with an oath, which put the fact beyond all doubt, that if one of those shot from the enemy had struck him, he never would have lived to tell the tale.

From my gallant comrade of the "Intrepid," we heard of the search that had been made in Wolstenholme Sound, and along the north shore of Lancaster Sound. In both places numerous traces of Esquimaux had been seen, at Wolstenholme Sound especially. These were numerous and recent, and the "Intrepid's" people were shocked, on entering the huts, to find many dead bodies; the friends, evidently, of our Arctic Highlander, Erasmus York, who, as I before said, had shipped as interpreter on board the "Assistance." In Wolstenholme Sound, the cairns erected by the "North Star" were discovered and visited, and, whilst speaking of her, it will be as well for me to note, that Captain Penny, on his way up Lancaster Sound, met the "North Star" off Admiralty Inlet, August 21st, gave Mr. Saunders his orders from England, and told him of the number of ships sent out to resume the search for Franklin. Captain Penny left Mr. Saunders under an impression that he was going to Disco, to land his provisions.

There was one remarkable piece of information, which I noted at the time, and much wondered at; it was derived from Captain Penny, and the officers of the "Lady Franklin" and "Sophia." It appears they crossed Wellington Channel, about ten miles higher up than we did; the ice breaking away, it will be remembered, and drifting with the "Resolute" and "Pioneer" to the south. From a headland about twelve miles north of Barlow Inlet, Captain Penny observed with astonishment that there was only about ten miles more of ice to the north of his vessels, and then, to use his own words, "Water! water! large water! as far as I could see! to the N. W." How this water came there? what was beyond it? were questions which naturally arose; but it was not until the following year that the mystery was explained, and we learned, what was only then suspected, that we had overshot our mark.

Sept. 11th, 1850.—The winter of the Arctic Regions came on us, in its natural character of darkness, gale, cold, and snow. First, the wind from the S. E., with a heavy sea, which sent us careering against the floe-edge, and gave all hands a hard night's work to keep the anchors in the firm floe, as the edge rapidly broke up, under the combined effects of sea and shocks from our vessels; then, with a gust or two, which threatened to blow the sticks out of our craft, the wind chopped round to the N. W.; and a falling temperature, which Arctic statistics told us would not, at this season, ever recover itself, said plainly, that winter quarters alone remained for us.

Happily, the "Intrepid" had discovered a harbour between Cape Hotham and Martyr, on the south side of Cornwallis Island. This place, and Union Bay, in Beechey Island, offered two snug positions, from which operations in the spring with travelling parties could be well and effectually carried out. Action, action now alone remained for us; and earnestly did we pray that our leader's judgment might now decide upon such positions being taken up as would

5*

secure all directions—viz. to the south-west,—north-west and, lastly, west being provided for.

Sept. 13*th*.—Found the four vessels of our squadron, and one of the American brigs,—the "Advance" under Lieutenant De Haven,—all safe at the floe-edge. The floe had drifted during the gale considerably towards the shores of North Somerset; and the wedge-shaped island, called Cape Bunny, was distinctly visible: the other of the American brigs had, in the height of the gale, blown adrift and disappeared in the darkness and snow-drift. For her, as well as Her Majesty's brigs under Captain Penny, much anxiety was entertained. The American leader of the expedition, I heard, finding farther progress hopeless, intended, in obedience to his orders, to return to New York. This he was the more justified in doing, as no preparation or equipment for travelling-parties had been made by them, and their fittings for wintering in the Arctic Regions were, compared with ours, very deficient. The gallant Yankees, however, could not return without generously offering us provisions, fuel, and stores; and the officers, with a chivalrous feeling worthy of themselves and the cause for which they had come thus far, offered to remain out or exchange with any of "ours" who wanted to return home. We had no space in stowage to profit by the first offer, nor had enthusiasm yet become sufficiently damped in us to desire to avail ourselves of the proffered exchange; both were declined, and it was said that Lieutenant De Haven was told by our leader, if he could land any thing for us in Radstock Bay as a dépôt, he might render good service.

Letters were therefore hurriedly closed, letter-bags made up, and pleasant thoughts of those at home served to cheer us, as, with the temperature at about zero, and with a fresh breeze, we cast off together, and worked to the northward, towards Griffith's Island.

Rubbing sides almost with the "Advance," who courteously awaited with the "Pioneer" the heavy-heeled gambols of the "Resolute," day was drawing on before the squadron reached Griffith's Island, from the lee of which the missing American schooner was descried to be approaching. Lieutenant De Haven now hoisted his colours for home, and backed his topsail. We did the same; and after a considerable time he bore up with his squadron for New York, doubtless supposing, from no letters being sent, that we had none.

It was far otherwise; and throughout the winter many a growl took place, as a huge pile of undespatched letters would pass before our sight, and blessings of a doubtful nature were showered on our ill luck.

To the ice, which extended unbroken from Griffith's Island to Cape Martyr, we will leave the Naval expedition secured, whilst we briefly recount the most striking points in connection with the American expedition that had now left us on its voyage home.

In 1849, Mr. Henry Grinnell, a merchant of the United States, actuated by the purest philanthropy that ever influenced the heart of man, determined to devote a portion of his well-deserved wealth to the noble purpose of relieving Sir John Franklin, who, it was much to be feared, from the desponding tone of a portion of the English press on Sir James Ross's failure, was likely to be left unsought for in 1850. He therefore, at his sole expense, purchased two vessels, one of 140 tons, the "Advance," the other 90 tons, the "Rescue," and, having strengthened, provisioned, and equipped them, Mr. Grinnell then placed them under the control of his Government, in order that they might be commanded by naval officers and sail under naval discipline. The American Congress passed the necessary acts, and Lieutenant E. De Haven, who had seen service in the Antarctic seas, took command of the "Advance," as the leader of the expedition, and another distinguished officer, Mr. Griffin, hoisted his pendant in the "Rescue." On the 23d May, 1850, the two vessels sailed from New York, touching at Disco, where I am sorry to say they found my worthy friend "Herr Agar" to have died shortly after my visit; they reached the pack of Melville Bay on the 7th July, and, tightly beset until the 23d, they did not reach Cape York until early in August.

The 7th August they reached Cape Dudley Digges! (at that time we were still beset off Cape Walker in Melville Bay), thence they stood to the south-west, until they reached the West Water.

On the 18th August, when we had a thick fog and almost a calm off Possession Bay, the American squadron was in a severe gale in Lancaster Sound; and on the 25th August, after visiting Leopold Island, the gallant Americans reached Cape Riley close on the heels of the "Assistance" and "Intrepid."

From that time we have shown that they lost no opportunity of pushing ahead; and if progress depended alone upon skill and intrepidity, our go-ahead friends would have given us a hard tussle for the laurels to be won in the Arctic regions.

As a proof of the disinterestedness of their motives, men as well as officers, I was charmed to hear that before sailing from America they had signed a bond not to claim, under any circumstances, the £20,000 reward the British Government had offered for Franklin's rescue; we, I am sorry to say, had acted differently. America had plucked a rose from our brows; but in such generous enterprise, we for the most part felt that no narrow-minded national prejudices could enter, and I gloried in the thought that the men who had so nobly borne themselves, as well as he, the princely merchant who had done his best to assist the widow and orphan to recover those for whom they had so long hoped and wept, were men who spoke our language, and came from one parent-stock—a race whose home is on the great waters.

Looking at my rough notes for the following week, I am now puzzled to know what we were hoping for; it must have been a second open season in 1850,—a sanguine disposition, no doubt brought about by a break in the weather, not unlike the Indian summer described by American writers.

September 14th.—I went in the "Pioneer," with some others, to see if the floe had opened a road to the south of Griffith's Island; it had not, nor did it appear likely to do so this season, though there was water seen some fifteen miles or so to the westward.

One day the "Assistance" and "Intrepid" started for Assistance Harbour, to winter there, but came back again, for winter had barred the route to the eastward as well as westward. One day after this, or rather, many days, we amused ourselves, with powder, blowing open a canal astern of the "Resolute," which froze over as quickly as we did it. At other times, some people would go on the top of the island, and see oceans of water, where no ship could possibly get to it, and then others would visit the same spot after a night or two of frost, and, seeing ice where the others had seen water, asserted most confidently that the first were exaggerators!

At any rate, September passed; winter and frost had undoubted dominion over earth and sea; already the slopes of Griffith's Island, and the land north of us, were covered with snow; the water in sight was like a thread, and occasionally disappeared altogether. Fires all day, and candles for long nights, were in general requisition. Some cross-fire in the different messes was taking place as the individuals suffered more or less from the cold. Plethoric ones, who became red-hot with a run up the ladder, exclaimed against fires, and called zero charming weather; the long and lethargic talked of cold draughts and Sir Hugh Willoughby's fate; the testy and whimsical bemoaned the impure ventilation. A fox or two was occasionally seen scenting around the ships, and a fox-hunt enlivened the floe with men and officers, who chased the unlucky brute as if they had all come to Griffith's Island especially for fox-skins; and the last of the feathered tribe, in the shape of a wounded "burgomaster," shivered, half frozen, as it came for its daily food.

October 2d, 1850.—Lieutenant M'Clintock had very properly urged the necessity of sending travelling parties to forward dépôts of provisions upon the intended routes of the different parties in 1851: these were this morning despatched, —Lieutenant M'Clintock, with Dr. Bradford, carrying out a dépôt towards Melville Island; Lieutenant Aldrich taking one to Lowther Island, touching at Somerville Island on the way.

Lieutenant Mecham was likewise sent to examine Cornwallis Island, between Assistance Harbour and Cape Martyr, for traces of Franklin.

We, who were left behind, felt not a little anxious about these parties whilst absent, for winter was coming on with giant strides; on the 4th, frost-bites were constantly occurring, and the sun, pale and bleary, afforded more light than warmth. Our preparations for winter were hurried on as expeditiously as possible; and the housing, which, like a tent, formed a complete covering to our upper decks, afforded great comfort and shelter from the cold bleak wind without.

On the 5th, Lieutenant Aldrich returned from his journey; he had not been able to go beyond Somerville Island—the sea between it and Lowther Island being covered with *broken packed ice, half-frozen sludge, and young ice.* On the 7th, Lieutenant Mecham arrived with the intelligence that the "Lady Franklin" and "Sophia" were, with the "Felix," safe in Assistance Harbour. Captain Penny, after his failure in reaching Cape Walker, had a narrow escape of being beset on the shores of North Somerset; but by carrying on through the pack, in the gale of the 11th September, he had happily secured his ships in excellent winter quarters.

Lieutenant Mecham had an adventure on his outward route, which had some interesting features: as he was crossing the entrance of a bay, since named Resolute Bay, he observed a bear amongst some hummocks, evidently breaking the young ice by a sort of jumping motion; and he then saw that he and his party had unconsciously left the old ice, and were travelling over bay-ice, which was bending with the weight of the men and sledge. Bruin's sagacity here served the seamen in good stead, and the sledge was expeditiously taken to firmer ice, whilst Mr. M. went in chase of the bear; having mortally wounded it, the brute rushed to seaward, and the sportsman only desisted from the pursuit when he observed the bear fall, and in doing so break through the ice, which was too weak to sustain its weight.

Captain Penny, on the following day, sent over his dog-sledge to secure the flesh for his dogs, by which time the unlucky bear was frozen to a hard and solid mass.

October 9th.—Lieutenant M'Clintock returned; he had placed his dépôt forty miles in advance, towards Melville

Island,—three days' imprisonment by bad weather, in the tents, having foiled his hopes of reaching Bedford Bay in Bathurst Island, where he originally intended to have reached. This party had, likewise, met water to the westward, and there was now but little doubt on our minds, that, had the large field of ice which was blocking the way between Cape Bunny and Griffith's Island broken up or drifted away, our squadron would have reached, in all probability, as far as Parry did in '20; but now, the utmost we could hope to attain in the following year was Melville Island, which would be our *goal*, instead of our *starting* point.

Autumn travelling differs, in some measure, from that of the spring. I will, therefore, give the indulgent reader an account of a short excursion I made for the purpose of connecting the search from where Lieutenant Mecham left the coast, to the point at which Lieutenant M'Clintock had again taken it up; in fact, a bay, facetiously christened by the seamen (who had learned that newly-discovered places were forbidden to be named), "Bay, Oh! no we never mention it!" and "Cape No Name."

My kind friend, Mr. May of the "Resolute," volunteered to accompany me, and on Thursday, the 10th of October, we started with our tent, a runner-sledge, and five days' provisions. The four seamen and our two selves tackled to the drag-ropes, and, with the temperature at 6° above zero, soon walked ourselves into a state of warmth and comfort.

Three hours' sharp dragging brought us to Cape Martyr; ascending the beach until we had reached a ledge of smooth ice which fringed the coast within the broken line of the tide-marks, we turned to the westward, and commenced searching the beach and neighbouring headlands. I shall not easily efface from my memory the melancholy impression left by this, my first walk on the desolate shores of Cornwallis

Island. Like other things, in time the mind became accustomed to it; and, by comparison, one soon learned to see beauties even in the sterility of the North.

Casting off from the sledge, I had taken a short stroll by myself along one of the terraces which, with almost artificial regularity, swept around the base of the higher ground behind, when, to my astonishment, a mass of stone-work, and what at first looked exactly like a cairn, came in view; it required no spur to make me hasten to it, and to discover I was mistaken in supposing it to have been any thing constructed so recently

Horizontal Section,
20 feet circumference.

Vertical Section,
5 feet 6 inches high.

as Franklin's visit. The ruin proved to be a conical-shaped building, the apex of which had fallen in. Its circumference, at the base, was about twenty feet, and the height of the remaining wall was five feet six inches. Those who had constructed it appeared well acquainted with the strength of an arched roof to withstand the pressure of the heavy falls of snow of these regions; and much skill and nicety was displayed in the arrangement of the slabs of slaty limestone, in order that the conical form of the building might be preserved throughout.

We removed the stones that had fallen into the building, but found nothing to repay our labour; indeed, from the quantity of moss adhering to the walls, and filling up the interstices of the masses which formed the edifice, I conjectured it was many years since it was constructed, though it would be impossible to guess when it was last inhabited; for, at Pond's Bay, I observed the remains of the native habitations to have the appearance of extreme old age and long abandonment, although, from the fresh seal-blubber *cachés*, there was not a doubt of the Esquimaux having been there the previous winter.

A mile beyond this ruin we halted for the night. Four of us (for, in Arctic travelling, officer and man are united by the common bond of labour) erected the tent over a space which we had cleared of the larger and rougher pieces of limestone, leaving what was called a soft spot as our castle and bedroom. One man, who dubbed himself cook for the day, with a mate, whose turn it would be to superintend the kitchen on the morrow, proceeded to cook the dinner. The cooking apparatus was a boat's stove, eighteen inches long, and nine inches broad, in which lignum vitæ was used as fuel.

Water having first to be made from ice and snow, and

then boiled in the open air, the process was not an expeditious one, and I took my gun and struck inland; whilst Mr. May, in an opposite direction, made for a point of land to the westward.

No pen can tell of the unredeemed loneliness of an October evening in this part of the polar world: the monotonous, rounded outline of the adjacent hills, as well as the flat, unmeaning valleys, were of one uniform colour, either deadly white with snow or striped with brown where too steep for the winter mantle as yet to find a holding ground. You felt pity for the shivering blade of grass, which, at your feet, was already drooping under the cold and icy hand that would press it down to mother earth for nine long months. Talk of "antres vast and deserts idle,"—talk of the sadness awakened in the wanderer's bosom by the lone scenes, be it even by the cursed waters of Judea, or afflicted lands of Assyria,—give me, I say, death in any one of them, with the good sun and a bright heaven to whisper hope, rather than the solitary horrors of such scenes as these. The very wind scorned courtesy to such a repulsive landscape, and as the stones rattled down the slope of a ravine before the blast, it only recalled dead men's bones, and motion in a catacomb. A truce, however, to such thoughts—May's merry recognition breaks the stillness of the frosty air. He has been to the point, and finds it an island; he says—and I vow he means what he says—that May Island is a beautiful spot! it has grass and moss upon it, and traces of game: next year he intends to bag many a hare there. Sanguine feelings are infectious; I forget my own impressions, adopt his rosy ones, and we walk back to our tent, guided by the smoke, plotting plans for shooting excursions in 1851!

"Pemmican is all ready, sir!" reports our Soyer. In troth, appetite need wait on one, for the greasy compound would pall on moderate taste or hunger. Tradition said that it was composed of the best rump-steaks and suet, and cost 1s. 6d. per pound, but we generally voted it composed of broken-down horses and Russian tallow. If not sweet in savour, it was strong in nourishment, and after six table-spoonfuls, the most ravenous feeder might have cried, hold! enough!

Frozen pork, which had been boiled on board the ship, was quite a treat, and decidedly better than cold, thawed pork could have been; this, with plenty of biscuit and a "jolly hot" basin of tea, and, as one of the seamen observed, "an invitation to Windsor would have been declined." The meal done, the tent was carefully swept out, the last careful arrangement of the pebbles, termed "picking the feathers," was made, and then a water-proof sheet spread, to prevent our warm bodies, during the night, melting the frozen ground and wetting us through. Then every man his blanket bag, a general popping thereinto of the legs and body, in order that the operation of undressing might be decently performed, the jacket and wet boots carefully arranged for a pillow; the wolf-skin robes,—Oh, that the contractor may be haunted by the aroma of the said robes for his life-time!—brought along both over and under the party, who lie down alternately, head and feet in a row, across the tent. Pipes are lighted, the evening's glass of grog served out; and whilst the cook is washing up, and preparing his things ready for the morning meal, as well as securing the food on the sledges from foxes, or a hungry bear, many a tough yarn is told, or joke made, which keep all hands laughing until the cook reports all right, comes in, hooks up the door, tucks in the fur robe; and seven jolly mortals, with a brown-holland tent over their heads, and a winter's gale without, try to nestle their sides amongst the softest stones, and at last drop into such a sleep as those only enjoy who drag a sledge all day, with the temperature 30° below freezing point.

Friday morning, at seven o'clock, we rolled up our beds, or rather sleeping-bags, stowed the sledge, drank boiling hot chocolate, and gnawed cheerily at frozen pork and biscuit; the weather beautiful, calm, and very cold, below zero, we started, skirting round the bay. By noon a gale sprung up, sending a body of icy spiculæ against our faces, causing both pain and annoyance. Two mock suns for the first time were seen to-day. At noon we sat down under the lee of our sledge, and partook of a mouthful of grog and biscuit, and again marched rapidly towards "Cape No Name!" By the evening we had marched fourteen miles, the entire circuit of the bay, without observing any trace of Franklin having visited the neighbourhood; and as frost-bites began to attack our faces, we erected our tent as expeditiously as possible, and in it took shelter from the wind and cold. The pungent smoke of the lignum vitæ kept us weeping, as long as the cooking went on; and between the annoyance of it, the cold, and fatigue, we all dropped off to sleep, indifferent to a falling temperature, prowling bears, or a violent gale, which threatened to blow us from the beach on which we had pitched our fluttering tent.

Next day, my work being done, we struck homeward for the squadron, and reached it the same evening, the said 12th of October being the last autumnal travelling of our squadron.

The following week the temperature rallied a little, and the weather was generally finer; our preparations for wintering were nearly completed, and the poor sickly sun barely for two hours a day rose above the heights of Griffith's Island.

To our great joy, on the 17th of October, Captain Penny

came over from Assistance Harbour. He had happily decided on taking up the search of Wellington Channel; and an understanding was come to, that his squadron should carry out the travelling operations next spring on that route, whilst our squadron accomplished the farthest possible distance towards Melville Island, and from Cape Walker to the south-west.

Captain P. expressed it as his opinion that the Americans had not escaped out of Barrow's Strait, in consequence of a sudden gale springing up from the southward, shortly after they had passed his winter quarters. This supposition we of course afterwards found to be true, although at the time we all used to speak of the Americans as being safe and snug in New York, instead of drifting about in the ice, within a few miles of us, as was really the case.

With Penny's return to his vessels, may be said to have closed all the Arctic operations of the year 1850. Our upper decks were now covered in; stoves and warming apparatus set at work; boats secured on the ice; all the lumber taken off the upper decks, to clear them for exercise in bad weather; masts and yards made as snug as possible; rows of posts placed to show the road in the darkness and snow-storms from ship to ship; holes cut through the ice into the sea, to secure a ready supply of water, in the event of fire; arrangements made to insure cleanliness of ships and crews, and a winter routine entered upon, which those curious in such matters may find fully detailed in Parry's "First Voyage," or Ross's "Four Years in Boothia."

The building of snow-walls, posts, houses, &c., was at first a source of amusement to the men, and gave them a great field in which to exercise their skill and ingenuity. People at home would, I think, have been delighted to see the pretty and tasteful things cut out of snow: obelisks, sphinxes, vases, cannon, and, lastly, a stately Britannia, looking to the westward, enlivened the floe, and gave voluntary occupation to the crews of the vessels. These, however, only served for a while; and as the arctic night of months closed in, every one's wits were exerted to the utmost to invent occupation and entertainment for our little community.

On November the 8th, two officers ascended the heights of Griffith's Island, and at noontide caught the last glimpse of the sun, as it happened to be thrown up by refraction, though in reality it was seventeen miles below our horizon. We were now fairly about to undergo a dark, arctic winter, in 74½ degrees of north latitude; and light-hearted and confident as we felt in our resources of every description, one could not, when looking around the dreary scene which spread around us on every side, but feel how much our lives were in His hands who tempers the wind to the shorn lamb; and wanting must he have been in feeling who did not offer up a heartfelt prayer that returning day and returning summer might find him able and fit to undergo the hardship and fatigue of journeys on foot, to seek for his long-lost fellow-seamen. On leaving England, amongst the many kind, thoughtful presents, both public and private, none struck me as being more appropriate than the following form of prayer:—

A PRAYER FOR THE ARCTIC EXPEDITION.

"O Lord God, our Heavenly Father, who teachest man knowledge, and givest him skill and power to accomplish his designs, we desire continually to wait, and call, and depend upon Thee. Thy way is in the sea, and Thy paths in the great waters. Thou rulest and commandest all things. We therefore draw nigh unto Thee for help in the great work which we now have to do.

"Leave us not, we beseech Thee, to our own counsel, nor

to the imaginations of our own foolish and deceitful hearts: but lead us by the way wherein we should go, that discretion may preserve us, and understanding may keep us. Do Thou, O Lord, make our way prosperous, and give us Thy blessing and good success. Bring all needful things to our remembrance; and where we have not the presence of mind, nor the ability, to perform Thy will, magnify Thy power in our weakness. Let Thy good providence be our aid and protection, and Thy Holy Spirit our Guide and Comforter, that we may be defended from all adversities which may happen to the body, and from all evil thoughts which may assault and hurt the soul. Endue us with such strength and patience as may carry us through every toil and danger, whether by sea or land; and, if it be Thy good pleasure, vouchsafe to us a safe return to our families and homes.

"And, as Thy Holy Word teaches us to pray for others, as well as for ourselves, we most humbly beseech Thee, of Thy goodness, O Lord, to comfort and succour all those who are in trouble, sorrow, need, sickness, or any other adversity, especially such as may now be exposed to the dangers of the deep, or afflicted with cold and hunger. Bestow upon them Thy rich mercies, according to their several wants and necessities, and deliver them out of their distress. They are known to Thee by name, let them be known of Thee as the children of Thy grace and love. Bless us all with Thy favour, in which is life, and with all spiritual blessings in Christ Jesus; and grant us so to pass the waves of this troublesome world, that finally we may come unto Thy everlasting kingdom. Grant this, for Thy dear Son's sake, Jesus Christ our Lord. *Amen.*"

While touching on a religious point connected with our expedition, I must say, that as yet we have not in the Navy a single good set of sermons adapted to interest and instruct the seamen. The commander, or commanding officer, of a man-of-war usually reads, in the absence of the chaplain, the Divine Service on Sundays. We, of course, did not fail to do so; but I never saw an English sailor who would sit down and listen attentively to the discussion of some knotty text, exhibiting far more ingenuity on the part of some learned commentator, than simplicity and clearness adapted to plain, uninformed minds: in a future expedition, and, indeed, in the Navy generally, it is to be hoped this deficiency will be remedied. Sermons in the pure and Christianlike tone of Porteus's Lent Lectures, I would humbly recommend as a guide for those who may be inclined to take the good work in hand.

A theatre, a casino, and a saloon, two Arctic newspapers, one of them an illustrated one, evening-schools, and instructive lectures, gave no one an excuse for being idle. The officers and men voluntarily imposed on themselves various duties in connection with the different departments; one was scene-painter, and under his talented pencil the canvas glowed with pictures one almost grieved to see thus employed. Decorators and statuaries produced effects which, with such limited means, were really astounding; vocalists and musicians practised and persevered until an instrumental band and glee-club were formed, to our general delight; officers and men sung who never sang before, and maybe, except under similar circumstances, will never sing again; maskers had to construct their own masks, and sew their own dresses, the signal flags serving in lieu of a supply from the milliner's; and, with wonderful ingenuity, a fancy dress ball was got up, which, in variety and tastefulness of costume, would have borne comparison with any one in Europe.

Here, editors floundered through a leader, exhibiting

French ingenuity, in saying their say without bringing themselves within the grasp of the censors; here, rough contributors, whose hands, more accustomed to the tar-brush than the pen, turned flowing sentences by the aid of old miscellanies and well-thumbed dictionaries. There, on wooden stools, leaning over long tables, were a row of serious and anxious faces, which put one in mind of the days of cane and birch,—an Arctic school. Tough old marines curving "pot-hooks and hangers," as if their very lives depended on their performances, with an occasional burst of petulance, such as, "D— the pen, it won't write! I beg pardon, sir; this 'ere pen will splutter!" which set the scholars in a roar. Then some big-whiskered top-man, with slate in hand, reciting his multiplication-table, and grinning at approval; whilst a "scholar," as the cleverest were termed, gave the instructor a hard task to preserve his learned superiority.

In an adjoining place, an observer might notice a tier of attentive, upturned faces, listening, like children to some nursery-tale. It was the first lieutenant of the "Resolute," my much-loved, faithful friend; he was telling them of the deeds of their forefathers in these regions. Parry's glorious pages open by his side, he told those stern men with tender hearts, of the sufferings, the enterprise, the courage, and the reward of imperishable renown exhibited and won by others. The glistening eye and compressed lip showed how the good seed had taken root in the listeners around, and every evening saw that sailor audience gather around him whom they knew to be the "gallant and true," to share in his feelings and borrow from his enthusiasm.

For some time after the sun had ceased to visit our heavens, the southern side of the horizon, for a few hours at noon, was strongly illumined, the sky being shaded, from deep and rosy red through all the most delicate tints of pink and blue, until, in the north, a cold bluish-black scowled angrily over the pale mountains, who, in widowed loneliness, had drawn their cowls of snow around, and, uncheered by the roseate kiss of the bridegroom sun, seemed to mourn over the silence and darkness at their feet. Such was a fine day in November, and through the gray twilight the dark forms of our people, as they traversed the floe, or scaled the cliffs of Griffith's Island, or, maybe, occasionally hunted a bear, completed the scene.

Charmed as we were with the evanescent colouring of our sky on a fine day, it was in loveliness far surpassed by the exceeding beauty of Arctic moonlight. Daylight but served to show the bleakness of frozen sea and land; but a full, silvery moon, wheeling around the zenith for several days and nights, threw a poetry over every thing, which reached and glowed in the heart, in spite of intense frost and biting breeze. At such a time we were wont to pull on our warm jackets and seal-skin caps, and, striding out upon the floe, enjoy to the utmost the elasticity of health and spirits with which we were blest under so bracing a climate. There, with one's friend, the mutual recognition of Nature's beauties and congratulations, at being there to witness it, richly rewarded us for our isolation from the world of our fellow-men; and general enthusiasm had its full sway as, from the heights of Griffith's Island, we looked down on our squadron, whose masts alone pierced the broad white expanse over Barrow's Strait, and threw long shadows across the floe. The noble mission for which they had been sent into the north was ever present to us, and away instinctively flew our thoughts to our gallant friends in the "Erebus" and "Terror:" thus alternately elated and saddened, we enjoyed, with earnest feelings, the wondrous scene around us.

Imagine yourself, dear reader, on the edge of a lofty table-land, which, dipping suddenly at your feet, sloped again to the sea of ice, at a distance of some 500 feet below; fancy a vast plain of ice and snow, diversified by tiers of broken-up ice and snow-wreaths, which, glistening on the one side, reflected back the moonlight with an exceeding brilliancy, whilst the strong shadow on the farther side of the masses threw them out in strong relief; four lone barks, atoms in the extensive landscape,—the observers' home,—and beyond them, on the horizon, sweeping in many a bay, valley, and headland, the coast of Cornwallis Island, now bursting upon the eye in startling distinctness, then receding into shadow and gloom, and then anon diversified with flickering shades, like an autumnal landscape in our own dear land, as the fleecy clouds sailed slowly across the moon,—she the while riding through a heaven of deepest blue, richly illuminated by the constellations of the northern hemisphere, wheeling around the Polar Star like armies in review,—and say if the North has not its charms for him who can appreciate such novel aspects of Nature.

If you still doubt it, let us descend the adjacent ravine, formed as if some giant hand had rent the firm cliff from crown to basement; stand we now at its upper entrance, where it slopes away to the table-land behind,—didst ever see a sight more wildly beautiful? The grim and frowning buttresses on either hand, too steep for even the snow-flake to rest upon, whilst over its brow a pigmy glacier topples with graceful curve, or droops in many an icy wreath and spray, threatening us with destruction as we slide down the sharp declivity. Now, with many a graceful curve, the gorge winds down to the frozen sea, a glimpse of which forms the background to the lower entrance. Observe how the snow, which, by wintry gales, has been swept into the ravine, has hardened into masses, resembling naught so much as a fierce rapid suddenly congealed; and then look overhead, to a deep blue sky, spangled with a million spheres; if thou couldst have seen this, and much more than pen or tongues can tell, and not admire it, then I say,

> "God help thee,
> Thou hast reason to be sad."

As late as the 18th of November, water, in a broad lane, was seen to the S. E. from the extreme of Griffith's Island, showing the pack to be in motion in Barrow's Strait, a belief we otherwise arrived at from the frequent appearance of a water-sky in the same direction, especially after spring-tides or strong N. W. gales. A few bears, perhaps eight in all, visited our ships during the closing period of 1850, showing they did not hibernate immediately the sun disappeared; indeed, so long as there was water near us, they would find seal, their usual, perhaps their only, food. And, apart from the appearance of water in our immediate neighbourhood, we were convinced that Lancaster Sound was still open, from the sudden rise of the temperature of the air, whenever the wind drew to that quarter; and, what was more extraordinary still, whenever the wind was from the northward, a black vapour, a certain indication of water, was seen to be rolling past Cape Hotham out of Wellington Channel: could that have been open so long after the sea in our neighbourhood was closed?

However, to return to the bears. Whenever an unlucky brute was seen, the severe competition as to who should possess his skin, entailed no small risk of life upon the hunters as well as the proprietor of the coveted prize; and crossing the line of fire was recklessly performed, in a manner to have shocked an "Excellent" gunner or a Woolwich artilleryman. Discretion was the better part of Ursine valour, and one brute was alone bagged, although a good many were very much frightened; the frequent chases, and constant failures, giving rise to much quizzing on the part of the unsportsmanlike, and learned dissertations by the Nimrods upon the rules to be observed in bear-shooting. As instances of what risks the community ran, whilst the furor for skins was at its height, I will merely say, that two unconscious mortals who had got on a hummock to see around, were mistaken in the twilight for bears, and stood fire from a rifle, which, happily for them, on this occasion, missed its mark; and one day, a respectable individual, trotting among the snow ridges, was horrified to see on a piece of canvas, in large letters, "Beware of spring-guns!" Picture to oneself the person's feelings. How was he to escape? The next tread of his foot, and, maybe, off into his body might be discharged the murderous barrel secreted for a bear. Fate decreed otherwise; the alarmed seaman escaped; and the spring-gun was banished to some lonely ravine, from which the proprietor daily anticipated a dead bear, and I, a dead shipmate; some of whom, pining for forlorn damsels at home, were led to sentimentalize in retired places.

My captain of the forecastle, whose sporting propensities I have elsewhere noted, cured me of a momentary mania for trophies of the chase, thus: a large bear and cub, after coming towards the "Pioneer," for some time halted, and were fired at by three officers with guns: of the three barrels only one went off, wounding the cub, which, with its mother, made for Griffith's Island. I chased, followed by some of the men, the foremost of whom was my ancient mariner, who kept close to my heels, urging me on by declaring we were fast catching the brutes. We decidedly had done so. By the time I reached the island, and both bears were within shot, climbing up, with cat-like agility, the steep face of the cliffs, again and again I failed to get my gun off; and as the she-bear looked at one time inclined to come down and see who the bipeds were that had chased her, I looked round at my supporters, who were vehemently exclaiming that "we should have her in a minute!" They consisted of Old Abbot, armed with a snow-knife, and some men who ran, because they saw others doing so. Now, a snow-knife consists of nothing more than a piece of old iron beaten out on an anvil so as to cut snow, having an edge, which, when I anxiously asked if it was sharp, I was figuratively told, "The owner, John Abbot, could have ridden to the devil upon it without injury to his person." Yet, with this, I verily believe, the old seaman would have entered the list against the teeth and talons of Mistress Bruin. I objected, however, and allowed her to escape with becoming thankfulness.

Christmas-day was, of course, not forgotten, and our best, though humble fare was displayed in each of the vessels. Hospitality and good-fellowship, however, were not confined to this day alone; and had not the bond of friendship, which knit the officers and men of the squadron together, taught them the necessity of sharing the little they had, the open-handed liberality of our hospitable leader would have done so. At his table, petty differences, professional heart-burnings, and quarter-deck etiquette, were forgotten and laid aside. A liberal and pleasant host made merry guests; and amongst the many ways in which we strove to beguile the winter of 1850–51, none have more agreeable recollections than his dinner-parties.

It may not here be out of place to describe the ordinary clothing worn, as yet, by officers and men: the temperature ranging often as low as 35° below zero, with strong gales:—

Clothing when indoors.

1 Flannel shirt with sleeves.
1 Cotton ditto.
1 Waistcoat with sleeves, lined with flannel.
1 Drawers flannel.
1 Pair trowsers, box-cloth, lined with flannel.
1 Pair thick stockings.
1 Do. thin ditto.
1 Horse-hair sole.
1 Pair carpet boots.

Additional for walking.

Box-cloth pea jacket.
Welsh wig.
Seal-skin cap.
Beaver-skin mitts.
Shawl or comfortable.
Men with tender faces required a cloth face-cover in the wind.

January, 1851.—That we were all paler, was perceptible to every one; but only a few had lost flesh. A very little exercise was found to tire one very soon, and appetites were generally on the decrease. For four hours a-day, we all, men and officers, made a point of facing the external air, let the temperature be what it would; and this rule was carefully adhered to, until the return of the sun naturally induced us to lengthen our excursions. Only on three occasions was the weather too severe for communication between the vessels, and the first of these occurred in the close of December and commencement of January. To show one's face outboard, was then an impossibility; the gale swept before it a body of snow higher than our trucks, and hid every thing a few yards off from sight. The "Resolute," three hundred yards off, was invisible; and the accumulation of snow upon our housing, threatened to burst it in. The floe seemed to tremble as the gale shrieked over its surface, and tore up the old snow-drifts and deposited them afresh. A wilder scene man never saw: it was worthy of the Arctic regions, and a fit requiem for the departing year.

After one of these gales, walking on the floe was a work of much difficulty, in consequence of the irregular surface it presented to the foot. The snow-ridges, called sastrugi by the Russians, run (where unobstructed by obstacles which caused a counter-current) in parallel lines, waving and winding together, and so close and hard on the edges, that the foot, huge and clumsy as it was with warm clothing and thick soles, slipped about most helplessly; and we, therefore, had to wait until a change of wind had, by a cross drift, filled up the ridges thus formed, before we took long walks; and on the road between the vessels parties were usually employed mending the roads.

With one portion of the phenomena of the North Sea, we were particularly disappointed—and this was the aurora. The colours, in all cases, were vastly inferior to those seen by us in far southern latitudes, a pale golden or straw colour being the prevailing hue; the most striking part of it was its apparent proximity to the earth. Once or twice the auroral coruscations accompanied a moon in its last quarter, and generally previous to bad weather. On one occasion, in Christmas-week, the light played about the edge of a low vapour which hung at a very small altitude over us; it never, on this occasion, lit up the whole under-surface of the said clouds, but formed a series of concentric semicircles of light, with dark spaces between, which waved, glistened, and vanished, like moonlight upon a heaving, but unbroken sea.

At other times, a stream of the same coloured vapour would span the heavens through the zenith, and from it would shoot sprays of pale orange colour for many hours; and then the mysterious light would again as suddenly vanish.

Clouds may have been said to have absented themselves from our sky for at least two months of the winter; the heavens, the stars, and moon, were often obscured, but it invariably appeared to be from snow-drift rather than from a cloudy sky. Snow fell incessantly, even on the clearest day, consisting of minute spiculæ, hardly perceptible to the eye, but which accumulated rapidly, and soon covered any thing left in the open air for a few minutes. With returning daylight, and the promise of the sun, clouds again dotted the southern heavens, and mottled with beautiful mackerel skies the dome above us.

The immense quantity of snow which in a gale is kept suspended in the air by the action of the wind, and is termed drift, quite astounded us; and on two occasions, with northwesterly gales, we had a good opportunity of noting its accumulation. The "Pioneer" and "Intrepid" laying across the wind, the counter-current caused a larger deposition around us than elsewhere. On the first occasion, after the wind subsided, we found a snow-wreath along the weather-side of the vessel for a length of one hundred and eighty feet, about eleven feet deep in the deepest part, and sloping gradually away for one hundred yards. After weighing a cubic foot of the snow, I calculated that, at the lowest computation, the mass thus deposited in twenty-four hours was not less than four hundred tons in weight! How the floe bore the pressure seemed unaccountable to me; but it did around the "Pioneer," although that near the "Intrepid" broke down, and the water flowed up above the snow, forming it rapidly into ice.

Much later in the winter—indeed in the month of March—a succession of furious gales quite smothered us; the drift piled up as high as the top of the winter housing, which was fifteen feet above the deck, and then blew over to leeward, filling up on that side likewise; whilst we, unable to face the storm without, could only prevent the housing from being broken in, by placing props of planks and spars to support the superincumbent weight. We had actually to dig our way out of the vessel; and I know not how we should have freed the poor smothered craft, had not Nature assisted us, by the breaking down of the floe. This at first threatened to injure and strain the "Pioneer," for, firmly held as she was all round, the vessel was immersed some two feet deeper than she ought to have been by the subsiding ice. We set to work, however, to try and liberate her, when one night a series of loud reports awakened me, and the quarter-master at the same time ran down to say, in his quaint phraseology, that "she was a going off!" a fact, of which there was no doubt, as, with sudden surges, the "Pioneer" overcame the hold the floe had taken of her poor sides, and after some time she floated again at her true water-line; while the mountain of snow around us had sunk to the level of the floe, and at first formed enormously thick ice; but this in time, by the action of the under-currents of warm water, reduced itself to the ordinary thickness of the adjoining floe.

Before we enter upon the subject of returning spring, and the new occupations and excitement which it called forth, let me try to convey an idea of a day spent in total darkness, as far as the sun was concerned.

Fancy the lower deck and cabins of a ship, lighted entirely by candles and oil lamps; every aperture by which external air could enter, unless under control, carefully secured, and all doors doubled, to prevent draughts. It is breakfast-time, and reeking hot cocoa from every mess-table is sending up a dense vapour, which, in addition to the breath of so many souls, fills the space between decks with mist and fog. Should you go on deck (and remember you go from 50° above zero to 40° below it, in eight short steps), a column of smoke will be seen rising through certain apertures called ventilators, whilst others are supplying a current of pure air. Breakfast done,—and, from the jokes and merriment, it has been a good one,—there is a general pulling on of warm clothing, and the major part of the officers and men go on deck. A few remain, to clean and clear up, arrange for the dinner, and remove any damp or ice that may have formed in holes or corners during the sleeping hours. This done, a muster of all hands, called "divisions," took place. Officers inspected the men, and every part of the ship, to see both were clean, and then they dispersed to their several duties, which at this severe season were very light; indeed, confined mainly to supply the cook with snow to melt for water, keeping the fire-hole in the floe open, and sweeping the decks. Knots of two or three would, if there was not a strong gale blowing, be seen taking exercise at a distance from the vessels; and others, strolling under the lee, discussed the past and prophesied as to the future. At noon, soups, preserved meats, or salt horse, formed the seamen's dinner, with the addition of preserved potatoes, a treat which the gallant fellows duly appreciated. The officers dined somewhat later—2 P. M. A little afternoon exercise was then taken, and the evening meal, of tea, next partaken of. If it was school night, the voluntary pupils went to their tasks, the masters to their posts; reading men producing their books, writing men their desks, artists painted by candle-light, and cards, chess, or draughts, combined with conversation, and an evening's glass of grog, and a cigar or pipe, served to bring round bed-time again.

Monotony was our enemy, and to kill time our endeavour: hardships there was none: for all we underwent in winter quarters, in the shape of cold, hunger, or danger, was voluntary. Monotony, as I again repeat, was the only disagreeable part of our wintering at Griffith's Island. Some men amongst us seemed in their temperament to be much better able to endure this monotony than others: and others who had no source of amusement—such as reading, writing, or drawing—were much to be pitied. Nothing struck one more than the strong tendency to talk of home, and England: it became quite a disease. We, for the most part, spoke as if all the most affectionate husbands, dutiful sons, and attached brothers, had found their way into the Arctic expeditions. From these maudlins, to which the most strong-minded occasionally gave way, we gladly sought refuge in amusements,—such as theatres and balls. To give an idea of the zest with which all entered these gayeties, I will recount a list of the characters assumed by the officers, at the first fancy dress ball.

Capt. Austin . . .	*Old Chairs to mend.*
Ommanney . .	*Mayor of Griffith's Island.*
Lieut. Aldrich . . .	*Fancy dress.*
Cator . . .	*Old English Gentleman.*
M'Clintock . .	*Blue Demon.*
Osborn . . .	*Black Domino.*
Brown . . .	*Red Devil.*
Mecham . .	*Blue and White Domino.*
Dr. Donnet . . .	*A Lady, then a Friar.*
Bradford . . .	*A Capuchin.*
Ward . . .	*A Beadle.*
Mr. King . . .	*Jockey.*
Rearse . . .	*Smuggler.*
May	*Roman Soldier.*
Hamilton . . .	*A Spinster.*
Eds	*Spanish Dancing Girl.*
Markham . . .	*As Allegory.*
Cheyne . . .	*Miss Maria.*
M'Dougall . .	*Vivandiere.*
Lewis . . .	*Farmer Wapstraw.*

Mr. Allard . . .	*Mahomet Ali.*
Webb . . .	*Bedouin Arab.*
Harwood . . .	*Miss Tabitha Flick.*
Allen . . .	*Greenwich Pensioner.*
Brooman . . .	*Punch.*
Crabbe . . .	*Sir Charles Grandison.*
Richards . . .	*A Scot.*

Whilst pirates, Turks, gipsies, and ghosts, without number, chequered the ball-room.

These our amusements; but the main object of our coming to the North was kept constantly in view, and nothing that labour or ingenuity could devise towards the successful accomplishment of our mission was wanting.

Some turned their attention to obtaining information for the general good, upon all that related to travelling in frozen regions; others plodded through many a volume, for meteorological information upon which to arrange a safe period of departure for the travellers in the spring; others tried to found some reasonable theory as to the geography of the unexplored regions around us; whilst a portion more actively employed themselves in bringing into action divers practical means of communicating with our missing countrymen which had been supplied to us in England.

Rockets, in the calm evenings of early winter, were fired with great effect; in proof of which, signals were several times exchanged, both in the autumn and spring, between Assistance Harbour and our squadron, by the aid of these useful projectiles, although the distance was twenty miles.

The balloons, however, as a more novel attempt for distant signalizing, or, rather, intercommunication, were a subject of deep interest. The plan was simple, and ingenious; the merit of the idea, as applicable to the relief of Sir John Franklin, by communicating to him intelligence of the position of the searching parties, being due to Mr. Shepperd, C. E. It was as follows: a balloon of oiled silk, capable of raising about a pound weight when inflated, was filled with hydrogen evolved from a strong cask, fitted with a valve, in which, when required for the purpose, a certain quantity of zinc filings and sulphuric acid had been introduced. To the base of the balloon, when inflated, a piece of slow match, five feet long, was attached, its lower end being lighted. Along this match, at certain intervals, pieces of coloured paper and silk were secured with thread, and on them the information as to our position and intended lines of search were printed. The balloon, when liberated, sailed rapidly along, rising withal, and, as the match burnt, the papers were gradually detached, and, falling, spread themselves on the snow, where their glaring colours would soon attract notice, should they happily fall near the poor fellows in the "Erebus" and "Terror."

Every care was taken to despatch these balloons with winds from the southward and south-east, so that the papers might be distributed to the north and north-west, and westward. Fire-balloons, of which there were a few, were likewise despatched; but the impression in my own mind is, that the majority of the balloons despatched by us, after rising to some height, were carried by counter-currents—always the most prevalent ones at the cold season of the year—to the southward and south-west. On two occasions I distinctly saw the balloons, when started with S. E. winds, pass for a while to the N. W., and then, at a great altitude, alter their course under the influence of a contrary current, and pass as rapidly to the S. E., in the teeth of the light airs we had on the floe.

The farthest distance from the point of departure at which any of these papers were found, as far as I know, appears to have been within fifty miles. The "Assistance" despatched some from near Barlow Inlet, which were picked up on the opposite side of Wellington Channel north of Port Innis. Neither this, however, nor our non-discovery of any papers during our travelling in 1851, can be adduced as a proof against their possible utility and success; and the balloons may still be considered a most useful auxiliary.

Next—indeed we should say before the balloons—as a means of communication, came carrier-pigeons. When first proposed, in 1850, many laughed at the idea of a bird doing any service in such a cause; and, maybe, might have laughed yet, had not a carrier-pigeon, despatched by Capt. Sir John Ross, from his winter quarters in 1850, actually reached its home, near Ayr, in Scotland, in five days. In our expedition none of these birds had been taken; but on board the "Felix" Sir John Ross had a couple of brace. I plead guilty, myself, to having joined in the laugh at the poor creatures, when, with feathers in a half-moulted state, I heard it proposed to despatch them from Beechey Island, in 74 degrees N. and 92 degrees W., to the meridian of Greenwich and 56 degrees N. latitude, even though they were slung to a balloon for a part of the journey. At any rate it was done, I think, on the 6th October, 1850, from Assistance Harbour. Two birds, duly freighted with intelligence, and notes from the married men, were put in a basket, which was attached to a balloon in such a manner, that, after combustion of a certain quantity of match, the carrier-pigeons would be launched into the air to commence their flight. The idea being that they would fetch some of the whaling vessels about the mouth of Hudson's Straits; at least so I heard. The wind was then blowing fresh from the north-west, and the temperature below zero.

When we in the squadron off Griffith's Island heard of the departure of the mail, the opinion prevalent was, the birds would be frozen to death. We were mistaken; for, in about one hundred and twenty hours, one of these birds, as verified by the lady to whom it had originally belonged, reached her house, and flew to the nest in which it had been hatched in the pigeon-house. It had, however, by some means or other, shaken itself clear of the packet entrusted to its charge. This marvellous flight of three thousand miles is the longest on record; but, of course, we are unable to say for what portion of the distance the bird was carried by the balloon, and when or where liberated; that depending upon the strength and direction of the gale in which the balloon was carried along.

Kites, which the kind Mr. Benjamin Smith had supplied me with, both as a tractile power to assist us in dragging sledges, as well as a means of signalizing between parties, afforded much interest, and the success of our experiments in applying them to dragging weights was so great, that all those I was able to supply gladly provided themselves with so useful an auxiliary to foot-travellers. Experience, however, taught us how impossible it was to command a fair wind, without which they were useless weight, and in severe weather there was some danger, when handling or coiling up the lines, of having to expose the hands and being frost-bitten.

My attempts failed to despatch the kites with a weight attached sufficient to keep a strain on the string, and so keep the kite aloft, whilst at the same time it was enabled to proceed through the air in any direction I chose; for, as may be conceived, a little too much weight made the kite a fixture, whilst a little too little, or a sudden flaw of wind, would topple the kite over and bring it to the earth. As a means of signalizing between ships when stationary, the flying of kites of different colours, sizes, or numbers, attached one to the other, would, I am sure, in the clear atmosphere of the Arctic regions, be found wonderfully efficacious.

Lastly, we carried out, more I believe from amusement than from any idea of being useful, a plan which had suggested itself to the people of Sir James Ross's expedition when wintering in Leopold Harbour in 1848–49, that of enclosing information in a collar, secured to the necks of the Arctic foxes, caught in traps, and then liberated. Several animals thus entrusted with despatches or records were liberated by different ships; but, as the truth must be told, I fear in many cases the next night saw the poor "postman," as Jack facetiously termed him, in another trap, out of which he would be taken, killed, the skin taken off, and packed away, to ornament, at some future day, the neck of some fair Dulcinea. As a "sub," I was admitted into this secret mystery, or otherwise, I with others might have accounted for the disappearance of the collared foxes by believing them busy on their honourable mission. In order that the crime of killing the "postmen" may be recognized in its true light, it is but fair that I should say, that the brutes, having partaken once of the good cheer on board or around the ships, seldom seemed satisfied with the mere empty honours of a copper collar, and returned to be caught over and over again. Strict laws were laid down for their safety, such as an edict that no fox taken alive in a trap was to be killed: of course no fox was after this taken alive; they were all unaccountably dead, unless it was some fortunate wight whose brush and coat were worthless: in such case he lived either to drag about a quantity of information in a copper collar for the rest of his days, or else to die a slow death, as being intended for Lord Derby's menagerie.

The departure of a postman was a scene of no small merriment: all hands, from the captain to the cook, were out to chase the fox, who, half frightened out of its wits, seemed to doubt which way to run; whilst loud shouts and roars of laughter, breaking the cold, frosty air, were heard from ship to ship, as the fox-hunters swelled in numbers from all sides, and those that could not run mounted some neighbouring hummock of ice, and gave a view halloo, which said far more for robust health than for tuneful melody.

During the darker period of the winter, and when the uncertainty of the weather was such that, from a perfect calm and clear weather, a few hours would change the scene to a howling tempest and thick drift, in which, if one had been caught, death must inevitably have followed, great care was necessary in taking our walks, to prevent being so overtaken; but, nevertheless, walks of seven or eight miles from the vessels were, on several occasions, performed, and a severe temperature faced and mastered with perfect indifference. I remember well on the 13th January seeing mercury, in a solid mass, with a temperature of 40° below zero, and being one of a good many who had taken three hours hard walking for mere pleasure.

We joked not a little at the fireside stories at home, of bitter cold nights, and being frozen to death on some English heath: it seemed to us so incredible that people should be frost-bitten, because the air was below freezing point; whilst we should have hailed with delight the thermometer standing at zero, and indeed looked forward to such a state of our climate, as people in the temperate zone would to May sunshine and flowers.

With the increasing twilight, many an anxious eye was cast from the top of Griffith's Island, to see the prospect of good foot-travelling offered by the floe: it cannot have been said to be cheering, for broken and hummocky ice met the eye whichever way one looked, with here and there a small smooth space; and if it looked so from the heights, we knew full well that when actually amongst those hummocks, the travelling would be arduous indeed. There was some time yet, however, to elapse before the tussle commenced; and many a snow-storm had time meanwhile to rage. With seamen's sanguineness, we trusted that they would fill up the hollows, and help to smooth over the broken pack; any way, we all knew "a long pull, a strong pull, and a pull altogether," would master more difficulties than as yet had shown themselves in the Arctic regions.

Such were our occupations, such the amusements, such the hopes and fears of our winter quarters off Griffith's Island; and looking back now at that period, we happily forget its dreariness, and recollect only its brighter moments—the fast friendship there formed for many, the respect and admiration for all.

February 7th, 1851.—The stentorian lungs of the "Resolute's" boatswain hailed, to say the sun was in sight from the mast-head; and in all the vessels the rigging was soon manned to get the first glimpse of the returning god of day. Slowly it rose, and loud and hearty cheers greeted the return of an orb whom the world, without the frozen zone, does not half appreciate, because he is always with them. For ninety-six days it had not gladdened us, and now its return put fresh life into our night-wearied bodies. For a whole hour we feasted ourselves with admiring the sphere of fire, which illumined without warming us; and, indeed, the cold now increased rather than otherwise, and our lowest temperature and severest weather did not occur until March.

Preparations for spring travelling were now hastened; daily committees of officers met, by order, to discuss every point, and receive, approve, or reject proposals and plans. Every soul, high and low, exerted his ingenuity and abilities to invent articles, portable and useful for travellers; whilst others sent in to the leader of the expedition schemes of search, in which distances, directions, weights, and material were duly considered. Hopes rose high, as every one felt that the field was thrown open to individual ability and skill. Every one, naturally, (for orders "to put the men in training" did not come out until afterwards,) commenced to "harden up" for the labour before them. Zealous individuals might be daily seen trying all sorts of patents. Out of their hard-earned wages some of the men bought and made sails of peculiar cut for their sledges; others, after the "working hours" were over, constructed water-bottles, velocipedes, cooking-tins; in fact, neither pains nor trouble were spared—officers and men vying in zeal.

Early in March an interchange of visits between our squadron and that under Captain Penny opened the communication. His vessels had got through the winter equally well with ourselves, and he, in like manner, was hard at work, preparing for the foot journeys; and, as no sledges or other equipment had been brought by him from England, in consequence of his hurried departure, every nerve had to be strained, and every resource called into existence, to enable him to overcome his difficulties in lack of material.

On the 8th of March, at 11 A.M., the temperature in the shade having been a couple of hours previously at 41° below zero, and mercury solid in the open air, we were delighted to see a solitary drop of water trickle down the black paint of the "Pioneer's" side: at that moment, oddly enough, the temperature in the shade was 36°—, and in the sun the thermometer only rose to 2° below zero! Water, however, it undoubtedly was, and as such we cheerfully hailed it, to prove the increasing heat of the sun, and to promise a coming summer. All March was a scene of constant business, diversified with sledge parades and amusing military evolutions, recalling to our minds unpleasant recollections of sweltering field-days and grand parades.

Having briefly touched upon the leading incidents connected with our winter, and brought events up to the preparations for a search on foot, it may not here be out of place to give a brief sketch of the causes which had brought about the necessity for so many Englishmen to be sojourning in these inclement regions, as well as occasioned the voyage of that distinguished navigator whose squadron we hoped to rescue.

The seamen of Northern Europe, the Norsemen and Scandinavians, seem, from the earliest records extant, to have sought for the glory attendant upon braving the perils of Polar Seas. From A. D. 860 to 982, from the sea-rover Naddod's discovery of Iceland, to Eirek "of the Red Hand's" landing on Greenland, near Hergolf's Ness, neither wreck, disaster, nor tempest, checked the steady, onward march of their explorations; robbing, as they eventually did a century afterwards, the immortal Genoese of one half his honours, by actually landing, under the pirate Biarni, on the new continent south of the river St. Lawrence.

In Greenland, a hardy race, the descendants of the Northland warriors, appear to have multiplied; for, in A. D. 1400, a flourishing colony stood on this threshold of the new world; converted to Christianity, the cathedral of Garda had been constructed, and the archives in Iceland proved it to have been successively held by no less than seventeen bishops; the colonies were known under the general terms of East and West Bygd (Bight), and numbered in all sixteen parishes, and two hundred and eighty farms, numerously populated.

Strict commercial monopoly, and the naturally secluded position of the Scandinavian colony in Greenland, seemed to have occasioned its perfect decadence, or, otherwise, as traditions tell us, a sudden hostile inroad of the Esquimaux swept off the isolated Europeans: from either cause there remained, after the lapse of two centuries, but the moss-covered ruins of a few churches, some Runic inscriptions, and the legends of the Esquimaux, who talked of a tall, fair-haired race, their giants of old.

The heirloom of the northern pirates, the dominion of the sea, passed, however, into England's hands, and with it that same daring love of the difficult and unknown, which had led the Viking from conquest to conquest: and whilst southern Europe sought for the wealth of the Indies in the more genial regions of the south, English seamen pushed their barks to the west, in the boisterous seas of high northern latitudes. Confining myself purely to those who essayed the passage to Cathay Cipango, and the Indies, by the north-west, first on the glorious scroll stands Frobisher. That sturdy seaman of Elizabeth's gallant navy, on the 11th of July, 1576, with three craft, whose united burden only amounted to *seventy-five tons*,—this "proud admiral" sighted the east coast of Greenland, in 61° north latitude. Unable to approach it for ice, which then, as now, hampers the whole of that coast, he was next blown by a gale far to the south-west on to the coast of Labrador, reaching eventually to 63° north latitude, and landing in Frobisher's Straits. He extricated his vessels with difficulty, and returned home, carrying a quantity of mica, which was mistaken for gold; and awakening the cupidity of the court, nobles, and merchants, three more expeditions sailed, exhibiting laudable courage and skill, but adding little to our geographical knowledge.

Such a succession of miscarriages damped the ardour for

north-west discovery for a while; until, in 1585, "divers worshipful merchants of London, and the West country, moved by the desire of advancing God's glory, and the good of their native land," equipped "John Davis" for a voyage of discovery to the unknown regions of the north-west.

Piteous as were his hardships—doleful as were his tales of the "lothsome view of ye shore, and ye irksome noyse of ye yce," "ye stinking fogs and cruelle windes" of Desolation Land—the seamen of that day seemed each to have determined to see and judge for himself, and ably were they supported by the open-handed liberality of wealthy private individuals, and the corporation of London merchants; whose minds, if we may judge of them by such men as Sir John Wolstanholme, Digges, Jones, and others, soared far above Smithfield nuisances and committees on sewers. After Davis we see Waymouth, then Hudson, who perished amid the scenes of his hardships and honours. Captains Button and Bylot, followed by the ablest, the first of Arctic navigators—Baffin,—he sweeping, in one short season, round the great bay which records his fame, showed us of the present day the high-road to the west; and did more; for he saw more of that coast than we modern seamen have yet been able to accomplish. Lastly, in that olden time, we have the sagacious and quaint Nor-West Fox, carrying our flag to the head of Hudson's Bay; whilst James's fearful sufferings in the southern extreme of the same locality, completed, for a while, the labours of British seamen in these regions.

A lull then took place, perhaps occasioned by the granting of a charter to certain noblemen and merchants in 1668, under the title of "Governor and Company of Adventurers of England," trading into Hudson's Bay, with the understanding that the discovery of a north-west passage was to be persevered in by them. During a century, they accomplished, by their servants, "Hearne and Mackenzie,"—the former in 1771, and the latter in 1789,—the tracing of the Copper-mine and the Mackenzie rivers to their embouchures into an arctic sea in the 70° parallel of north latitude; whilst a temporary interest, on the part of Great Britain, during the reign of George the Third, occasioned two names, dear to every seaman's recollection, to be associated with the accomplishment of geographical discovery in the same direction: the one was Nelson, who served with Captain Phipps, afterwards Lord Mulgrave, in his attempt to pass over the Pole; and the other, the greatest of English navigators—Cook, who, in 1776, failed to round the American continent by coming to the eastward from Behring's Straits.

At the commencement of the current century, our knowledge of the northern coast of the American continent amounted to a mere fraction. On the west, Cook had hardly penetrated beyond Behring's Straits; and on the east, Hudson's and Baffin's Bay formed the limit of our geographical knowledge; except at two points, where the sea had been seen by Hearne and Mackenzie.

Shortly after the Peace, one whose genius and ability were only to be equalled by his perseverance, the late Sir John Barrow, Secretary of the Admiralty, turned his attention to Arctic discovery, and especially the north-west passage. He had himself been to Spitzbergen, and as far north as the 80th parallel of latitude. Combating the prejudiced, convincing the doubtful, and teaching the ignorant, he awakened national pride and professional enterprise in a cause in which English seamen had already won high honours, and Great Britain's glory was especially involved. What difficulties he mastered, and how well he was seconded by others, and none more so than by the enlightened First Lord of the Admiralty, Viscount Melville, Sir John Barrow himself has told, in the able volumes which imperishably chronicle the deeds of ancient and modern explorers in Polar regions. Since 1818, with the exception of Sir John Ross's first voyage, we may have been said to have constantly added to our knowledge of the north-west.

It was in 1819 that Parry sailed to commence that magnificent series of discoveries which, since completed by Franklin, Richardson, Beechey, the Rosses, Back, Simpson, and Rae, have left us, after thirty-five years of well-spent toil and devotion, in perfect possession of the geographical features of Arctic America, and added *three thousand six hundred and eighty miles* of coast-line to our Polar charts. Is this nothing? If the mere *quid pro quo* is required of public servants, surely the Arctic navigator has far better repaid to his country the pay and food he has received at her hands than those who, in a time of universal peace, idle through year after year of foreign service in her men-of-war; and most assuredly, if we are proud of our seamen's fame and our naval renown, where can we look for nobler instances of it than amongst the records of late Arctic voyages and journeys. The calm, heroic sufferings of Franklin,—always successful, let the price be what it would; the iron resolution of Richardson; Back's fearful winter march to save his comrades; the devoted Hepburn, who, old though he be, could not see his former leader perish without trying to help him, and, whilst I write these lines, is again braving an Arctic winter in the little "Prince Albert;" Parry, who knew so well to lead and yet be loved; James Ross, of iron frame, establishing, by four consecutive years of privation and indomitable energy, that high character which enabled him to carry an English squadron to the unvisited shores of Victoria Land at the southern pole; and lastly, the chivalrous men, who, again under Franklin, have launched, in obedience to their Queen and country, into the unknown regions between the Atlantic and Pacific Oceans, to execute their mission or fall in the attempt.

It was to save these devoted servants, that the spring of 1851 saw full 500 British and American seamen within the frigid zone. That portion of them that had come by Baffin's Bay had been so far successful in their mission, that they had dispelled all the visions—gratuitous enough—of Franklin having perished by shipwreck or other disaster in his passage across the bay.

We had seen his winter quarters; we had seen his look-out posts, and the trail of his explorations. They all said, Onward! To be sure, we did not at once know by which route he had gone onward. The uncertainty, however, gave a spur to those about to be engaged in the searching parties, and each man thought there were especial reasons for believing one particular route to be the true one. The majority—indeed all those who gave the subject any consideration—believed Franklin to have gone either by Cape Walker, or to the north-west by Wellington Channel.

Hope, thank God, rode high in every breast, and already did the men begin to talk of what they would do with their new shipmates from the "Erebus" and "Terror" when they had them on board their respective ships: and I have no doubt they would have done as one gallant fellow replied, when I asked him if he thought himself equal to dragging 200 lbs., "O yes, sir, and Sir John Franklin too, when we find him."

Increasing light, decreasing cold, plenty to do, and certain anticipations upon each man's part, that he would be the fortunate one to find and save Franklin, made the month of April come in on us before we had time to think of it, but not before we were ready.

The original intention was for the sledges to have started

on the different routes laid down by our commodore on the 8th of April; but a fall of temperature on the 6th altered this plan, and a delay of one week was decided upon. I therefore availed myself of the occasion to visit Captain Penny's winter quarters; proceeding there on the dog-sledge of Mr. Petersen, who happened to be on board our vessel at the time.

Nothing, I conceive, can be more exhilarating than dog-sledging in the Arctic regions on a fine day, especially when, as in my case, the whole affair has the charm of novelty. The rattling pace of the dogs, their intelligence in choosing the road through the broken ice; the strict obedience paid by the team to one powerful dog whom they elect as leader; the arbitrary exercise of authority by the said leader; the constant use of the whip, and a sort of running conversation kept up by the driver with the different dogs, who well knew their names, as in turn Sampson! Caniche! Foxey! Terror! &c., &c., were duly anathematized, afforded constant amusement; apart from Petersen's conversation, which was replete with interest, and the information he gave me of the distances accomplished on the coast of Greenland by the Danes with dog-sledges, made me regret much we had not provided ourselves with a team or two for accomplishing any necessarily rapid journey.

When Mr. Petersen, at Uppernavik, had so nobly thrown up an appointment under the Danish crown to serve as interpreter with Penny in the search for Franklin, he brought with him a sledge and a few dogs: these had twice littered, and the numerous puppies were already grown into serviceable dogs, forming two efficient teams. The major part of the winter, scarcity of food, such as seal and bear, had told severely upon the poor creatures; but an Esquimaux dog lives on little when not worked; and, with a little oatmeal and grease, they had all outlived the severe season; and some bear's flesh having been luckily procured, there was every probability of good service being rendered by them. Our rate of travelling was over five miles per hour, and though making a considerable détour to avoid broken ice, I was shaking Penny by the hand four hours after leaving the "Pioneer:" the distance between the squadrons being about twenty miles in a straight line.

I was much struck with the great advantage of wintering in harbour, and near the shore, over a position, such as our squadron's, in the midst of the floe. There was a cheerfulness in the vicinity of the land, barren though it was, quite refreshing to one who had always a mile to walk during the winter to reach Griffith's Island, or remain satisfied with the monotony of the ice-field around the "Pioneer." Besides being snug in harbour, Captain Penny, satisfied of the security of his vessels, intended to leave only one man in each of them,—every other soul being told off for sledge-parties,—whereas our squadron would have some sixty men and officers left behind to take care of them, exposed as they were to be swept into Barrow's Strait, or farther, by any sudden disruption of the ice. I, therefore, mentally gave my adhesion to the opinion expressed by authorities at home, to secure winter quarters in some bay or harbour, and not to winter in the pack, unless it is unavoidable.

The oldest English officer who had ever wintered within the Arctic circle on a voyage of discovery, Sir John Ross, was not likely to be forgotten by me; and I sincerely congratulated the veteran on his escape from sickness during the past winter: and, though a wonderful instance of physical endurance, I, with others, could not but feel regret that a Naval officer so advanced in years, and who had served so long, should be necessitated to undergo privations, of which those who did not witness them can form no conception.

Time enabled me to do little more than admire the perseverance displayed by Capt. Penny, his officers and men, in their preparations for travelling. Sledges, cooking apparatuses, tents, in short, every thing was ready, having been made by themselves in the course of the winter; and, on the 13th April, six sledges, drawn by seamen, with an officer to each, and provisioned for forty days, would start for Wellington Channel, there to part into two divisions,—Capt. Stewart, of the "Sophia," taking the one side of the Channel, whilst Capt. Penny, with two extra dog-sledges, would direct the search in general. Delighted with all the arrangements, and equally so with the high spirit of chivalrous devotion apparent in every word and action of these our gallant coadjutors in the purest of enterprises, my heart was full as I said "Good-bye" to my hospitable friend Penny, on the 11th of April; and a rapid drive by Mr. Petersen carried me to the "Pioneer" in less than three hours. After a short halt, Mr. P. returned to Assistance Harbour, doing full forty miles, within twelve hours, on his dog-sledge.

I was astonished to find, on my return, that as yet the temperature at our winter quarters had not been registered as being above zero; whereas, in Assistance Harbour, Capt. Penny's quarters, the thermometer had occasionally for the past week ranged above it, and on the day before I left showed 11° in the shade. This difference of temperature was, doubtless, occasioned by the radiation of heat from the land, by which they were, unlike ourselves, surrounded.

During my absence, I was told that Mr. M'Dougal, of the "Resolute," who had been despatched as early as the 4th April to inspect the dépôts formed in the autumn, had returned to the ships, and brought accounts of a wholesale destruction of the one on Somerville Island, by bears. Hunger and mischievousness seemed alike to have induced the brutes to break and tear to pieces what they could not possibly eat—such as tins of patent chocolate, some of which were fairly bitten through. This information induced us all to take extra precautions in securing the provisions, of which dépôts during the march were to be formed.

It is now time to describe the sledges and their equipment, upon the completeness of which the lives of our travellers so entirely depended.

The sledges, constructed of tough and well-seasoned wood, had been carefully constructed in Woolwich Dockyard. They were shod with iron, and the cross-bars or battens which connected the two runners, and formed the floor upon which the load was placed, were lashed in their places by us when required for use. At the four corners of the sledges light iron stanchions dropped into sockets, and formed the support for the sides of a species of tray or boat, capable of serving to ferry the sledge crew across water in an emergency, as well as to keep the provisions and clothing in it dry. This boat was made in some cases of gutta-percha, in others of oiled canvas;—

	lbs.
And, together with the sledge and drag-ropes, which were made of horse-hair, to prevent their becoming hard and brittle from frost, weighed	120
Two fur blankets and spare blanket, two weighed . .	40
Nine blanket-bags for sleeping in	42
A tent of oblong form, made of a species of brown holland, supported by four boarding-pikes, and a line which served as a ridge-rope, and was set up to any heavy thing that came to hand	55
Mackintosh floor-cloth to spread over the snow or gravel .	12
A shovel to dig out snow for banking-up with . . .	5½

	lbs.
A cooking apparatus, invented by Lieutenant M'Clintock, capable of cooking a pint apiece of tea, cocoa, or pemmican, with a spirit lamp, tallow lamp, and spare kettle	17
Sextant, 1 gun, and gear	10
A bag containing 5 tin pannikins and 5 spoons . . .	5
A knapsack for each man, containing 1 flannel shirt, 1 Guernsey frock, 1 serge frock, 1 pair of drawers, flannel, 1 pair of boot hose, 1 pair of stockings, 2 pairs of blanket-socks, 1 towel, 1 comb, 1 lb. soap	48
Spare boots, and thick Guernsey frocks for sleeping in .	36
A tin case, containing pepper, salt, herbs dried, lucifer matches, grog-measure, calico and flannel bandages, plaster adhesive, lint, liniment, eye-wash, pills, simple ointment, glycerine, lancet, tincture of opium, pins, needles, and thread	16
Store-bag, containing broom or brush for sweeping the tent down with, spare boot-soles, wax, bristles, twine, shoe-tacks, crape awls, slow-match, nettle stuff, and strips of hide, cylinders for documents, printed records	11
Spare ammunition, cleaning rods, and wrench	14
Kites and string	12½
Dead weight, lbs.	440

Such were the weights of the sledge equipment in the case of one of those intended for a long journey. Nothing, it will be seen, was forgotten, and there was nothing superfluous; yet, as the 440 lbs. had to be dragged by six men, there was already 73 lbs. per man, which would, from its nature, be hardly any lighter at the end of the journey; and as about 200 lbs. was judged to be as much as a man could drag, there only remained 172 lbs. per man available for provision and package.

The daily scale of provision, as ordered by Capt. Austin, during the journeys, was to be as follows:—

Pemmican	1 lb.
Boiled pork	6 oz.
Biscuit	12 oz.
Rum, concentrated	¾ gill.
Tobacco	½ oz.
Biscuit dust	1 oz.
Tea and sugar	¾ oz.
Chocolate and sugar (alternate days) . . .	1¾ oz.
Lime-juice (for 10 days)	½ oz.

The fuel allowed to cook this, for a party of seven men, amounted to one pint and one gill of spirits of wine, or one pound eight ounces of tallow.

A little calculation soon showed that about forty days' provision was as much as any one sledge could take with it, or for an outward journey of about twenty days; which, at an average distance of ten miles per diem, would only give an extent of coast-line examined by any one sledge of two hundred miles.

Before I endeavour to show how, by a system of dépôts and relays, greater distances were achieved, the complete load of a long-party sledge may as well be shown.

	lbs.
Total dead weight	440
Pemmican and cases	330
Biscuit and dust, &c.	278
Pork and packages	123
Tea, sugar, chocolate, tobacco, &c., in a case	47
Lime-juice and rum	67
Spirits of wine and tallow	78
Sundries, tins, &c.	45
Number of men to drag, 7 .	1408

201 lbs. per man.

7*

The officer's load consisted of a gun, powder and ball, telescope, compass, and note-book; and as all the party, in anticipation of cold weather, had to be heavily clad, it may be supposed that the total weight to be dragged through snow and over rough ice was quite as much as the stoutest physical powers were capable of. Several days previous to departure we had travelled short journeys, in perfect marching order, and sledges ladened,—an arrangement which was highly beneficial; and from the way the sledges went over the floe, they gave us high hopes of answering our expectations in the forthcoming march.

From head-quarters the following arrangement of sledges was made public:—

Capt. Erasmus Ommanney was to cross Barrow's Strait to Cape Walker, with the following sledges and officers under his orders: he there was to use his own judgment as to the disposal of the force, it being required, in the event of two routes showing themselves, viz., one to the S. W., and the other W., that Lieut. Sherard Osborn was to be ordered to take up the latter.

GRAND SOUTHERN SEARCH.

Long-party sledge .	Reliance	*Domine dirige nos* . . .	Captain Ommanney, six men.
Ditto ditto .	True Blue	*Nil desperandum* . . .	Lieutenant Osborn, seven men.
Supporting sledge .	Succour	*Sequor juvare* . . .	Lieut. G. F. Mecham, six men.
Ditto ditto .	Enterprise	Gaze where some distant speck a sail implies, With all the thirsting gaze of enterprise.	Lieut. W. H. Browne, six men.
Ditto ditto . to Lieutenant Osborn	Adventure	Nothing adventure, nothing win	Mr. Vesey Hamilton (mate), seven men.
Ditto ditto .	Inflexible	*Respice finem* . . .	Mr. Charles Ede (assist. surg.), six men.
Ditto ditto . .	Success	One and all	Mr. F. S. Crabbe (2d master), seven men.

To the highly important direction northward up the unknown channel of Byam Martin Island, and which, as Lieut. Aldrich very properly thought, would intercept the course of Franklin, should he, from Wellington Channel, have sailed north about for Behring's Straits, two sledges were told off under that officer:—

Long-party sledge .	Lady Franklin	Faithful and firm . .	Lieut. R. D. Aldrich, 7 men.
Supporting sledge .	Hotspur . .	In Deo confide . .	Mr. R. R. Pearse (mate), 7 men.

Lastly to Melville Island, on which route a dépôt, forty miles in advance, had already been placed in the autumn, and renewed in the spring, the following party was appointed: Lieut. M'Clintock, on his reaching the said island, acting as he should judge fit as to despatching Mr. Bradford along the northern shores, whilst he prosecuted the search to and beyond Winter Harbour:—

Long-party sledge .	Perseverance	*Persevere to the end* .	Lieut. M'Clintock, 6 men
Do.	Resolute .	St. George and merry England Onward to the rescue	Dr. Bradford, 6 men.
Supporting sledge .	Excellent .	Respice, prospice	Mr. W. May (mate), 6 men.
Do.	Dasher . .	Faithful & intrepid	Mr. Shellabear (2d master), 6 men.
Do.	Parry . .	Endeavour to deserve	Mr. Cheyne (mate), 7 men.

Mr. M'Dougal, I have before said, started during the first week of April with his sledge, the "Beaufort,"—

That future pilgrims of the wave may be
Secure from doubt, from every danger free.

He had to replenish the dépôt formed for Lieut. M'Clintock, and then to connect the search round a deep bay, which connected Bathurst and Cornwallis Lands, for separate islands they were proved by him no longer to be.

Thus fifteen sledges, manned by one hundred and five men and officers, were equipped for the search, leaving on board the four vessels of the squadron, seventy-five souls, which number was afterwards further reduced by Mr. R. C. Allen being sent to search the islands to the westward with the sledge "Grinnell" and seven men.

It now only remains for me to show in what manner it was proposed to enable the supporting sledges to apply their resources, so that the long-parties should reach far beyond the two hundred miles, or twenty days' journey, of which they were alone capable when dependent on their own provision.

The plan proposed in the southern division will give the best idea. The supporting sledge "Success" was capable of feeding all the division for five days, by which time we hoped to be at Cape Walker, and then have sufficient to return back to the squadron, where it could again replenish, and, returning to the same point at which we had separated from it, form such a dépôt that each of the sledges in return would find five days' provisions to carry them home. By this means six out of the seven sledges in the southern search will be seen to reach a point fifty miles from their original starting-point in perfect condition so far as their provisions are concerned.

We will, for the sake of clearness, cause these six sledges to divide into three divisions, of two each, viz., a long-party sledge and a support: in each case the support can feed the long party for ten days, and then, forming a dépôt of provisions equal to ten days more, have sufficient left to reach back to Walker, and thence home. The long party are now still complete, after receiving two supports, equal to fifteen days, or 150 miles; and two dépôts stand in their rear, the one for ten days, the other for five days. The long party now starts, consuming its own provision (forming its own dépôts for the returning march), advances for twenty days, and accomplishes 200 miles; which, with that done whilst supported, makes in all a journey outward of thirty-five days, or 350 miles from the ships. Of course, with an increased number of supports, this distance and time may be carried on as long as the strength of the men will endure, or the travelling season admit of.

On the 12th of April, the day calm and cold, some 50° below freezing-point, a scene of bustle and merriment showed that the sledges were mustering previous to being taken to the starting-point, under the north-west bluff of Griffith's Island, to which they marched with due military pomp in two columns, directed by our chiefs. Our sense of decorum was constantly overthrown by the gambols of divers dogs, given to us by Captain Penny, with small sledges attached to them, on which, their food duly marked and weighed, with flags, mottoes, &c., in fact, perfect fac-similes of our own, were racing about, entangling themselves, howling for assistance, or else running between the men's legs and capsizing them on the snow, amidst shouts of laughter, and sly witticisms at the *tenders*, as they were termed. Reaching the halting-place, tents were pitched, luncheon served out, and all of us inspected, approved of, ordered to fall in, a speech made, which, as was afterwards remarked, buttered us all up admirably; the thanks of our leader given to Mr. M'Clintock, to whose foresight, whilst in England, and whose valuable information collated during his travelling experience under Sir James Ross, we were so entirely indebted for the perfect equipment we now had with us.

The inspection over, we trudged back to our ships, Sunday being spent by the men in cooking and eating, knowing as they did that there were a good many banian days ahead, packing up and putting away their kits, and making little arrangements in the event of accidents to themselves. Monday was no day for a start; but on the evening of the 15th April the breeze slackened, and the temperature only some 14° below freezing-point, we donned our marching attire, girded up our loins, and all hands proceeded to the sledges.

As we shut in our wooden homes with a projecting point of Griffith's Island, the weather suddenly changed, and a fast increasing breeze enveloped us in snow-drift. Reaching the sledges, and shaking them clear from the snow of the last two days, a hasty cup of tea and a mouthful of biscuit were partaken of, a prayer offered up, beseeching His mercy and guidance whose kind providence we all knew could alone support us in the hazardous journey we were about to undertake; hearty farewells, in which rough jokes covered many a kindly wish towards one another; and then, grasping their tracking lines, a hundred hoarse voices joined in loud cheers, and the divisions of sledges, diverging on their different routes, were soon lost to one another in snow and mist.

An April night, with its gray twilight, was no match for the darkness of a snow-storm from the S. W., and we had almost to feel our road through the broken ice off the bluffs of Griffith's Island.

At two o'clock in the morning we reached much piled-up ice; and in the hope of clearer weather in the evening, the word to halt and pitch the tents was given. The seven sledges of the division, picking out the smoothest spots, were soon secured. The tents fluttering in the breeze, a little tea cooked, short orders given, and then each man got into his blanket-bag, and dreamed of a fine day and finding Sir John Franklin.

In the evening the weather was still thick as pea-soup, with a double-reef topsail breeze blowing in our teeth; but detention was impossible, so we again packed up after a meal of chocolate and biscuit, and facing towards Cape Walker, we carried the hummocks by storm. Ignorance was bliss. Straight ahead, over and through every thing, was the only way; and, fresh, hearty, and strong, we surmounted tier after tier, which more light and a clearer view might only have frightened us from attempting. Here, a loud cheer told where a sledge had scaled the pile in its path, or shot in safety down the slope of some huge hummock. There, the cry, one! two! three! haul! of a party, and quizzical jokes upon name, flag, or motto, betokened that "Success" or "True Blue" had floundered into a snow-wreath, above which the top of the sledge-load was only to be seen, whilst seven red-faced mortals, grinning, and up to their waists in snow, were perseveringly endeavouring to extricate it; officers encouraging, and showing the way; the men labouring and laughing. A wilder or more spirit-stirring scene cannot be imagined.

A hard night's toil cleared all obstacles, and nothing but a fair, smooth floe was before us, sweeping with a curve to the base of Cape Walker; but a fresh difficulty was then met with, in the total absence of hummock or berg-piece, by which to preserve a course in the thick, foggy weather, that lasted whilst the warm south wind blew. Imagine, kind reader, a grayish haze, with fast-falling snow, a constant wind in the face, and yourself trying to steer a straight course where floe and sky were of one uniform colour. A hand dog-vane was found the best guide, for of course it was impossible to keep a compass constantly in hand; and the officers forming in a line ahead, so as just to keep a good sight of one another, were followed by the sledges, the crews of which soon learned that the easiest mode of travelling, and most equal division of labour, consisted in marching directly after one another; and as the leading sledge had the extra work of forming the road through the snow, and straining the men's eyes in keeping sight of the officers, the foremost sledge was changed every half hour or hour, according to their will.

It will be seen that we travelled by night, and hoped by such means to avoid the glare of the sun, and consequent snow-blindness. It entailed, however, at this early season of the year, great suffering in the shape of cold, the people being exposed to the weather during the severest part of the day. From the 15th to the 19th the weather was of the same nature,—constant gales of wind in our faces, snow-storms, and heavy drift; against which we struggled, helped by a rising temperature, that we flattered ourselves would end in summer,—a mistake for which we afterwards suffered bitterly, the men having, from the ease with which they kept themselves warm, become careless of their clothing, and heedless of those precautions against frost-bite which a winter's experience had taught them.

Easter Sunday came in gloomily, with a wind inclined to veer to the northward, and with every appearance of bad weather. Setting our sails on the sledges, and kites likewise when the wind served, the division hurried on for Cape Walker, which loomed now and then through the snow-drift ahead of us. The rapidity of the pace at which we now advanced—thanks to the help afforded by the sails—threw all into a profuse perspiration, especially the seamen, who really looked as if toiling under a tropical sun rather than in an arctic night, with the temperature below freezing-point. Fatigue obliged us to halt short of the land, and postpone for another day's march the landing on the unvisited shores of Cape Walker.

During the sleeping hours, the increased attention to the fur covering, and the carefully closed door, told us that the temperature was falling; and the poor cook, with a rueful countenance, announced that it was below zero, as he prepared the morning meal. More than usual difficulty was found in pulling on our stiffly-frozen boots, stockings, and outer garments; and when the men went out of the tent they soon found their clothing becoming perfectly hard, from the action of the intense cold on what had been for several days saturated with perspiration. To start and march briskly was now the only safety, and in double-quick time tents were down and sledges moving. A nor'-wester was fast turning up, and as the night of Easter Monday closed around us, the cold increased with alarming rapidity. One of those magnificent conglomerations of halos and parhelia common to these regions lit up the northern heavens, and, by the brilliancy of colouring and startling number of false suns, seemed as if to be mocking the sufferings of our gallant fellows, who, with faces averted and bended bodies, strained every nerve to reach the land, in hopes of obtaining more shelter than the naked floe afforded from the nipping effects of the cutting gale. Every moment some fresh case of frost-bite would occur, which the watchful care of the officers would immediately detect. The man would fall out from his sledge, restore the circulation of the affected part, generally the face, and then hasten back to his post. Constant questions of "How are your feet?" were heard on all sides, with the general response, "Oh! I hope they are all right; but I've not felt them since I pulled my boots on."

One halt was made to remove and change all leather boots, which, in consequence of our late warm weather, had been taken into use, but were now no longer safe; and then, with a rally, the piled-up floe around the cliffs of Cape Walker was reached. Cold and hungry as we were, it must have been a heavy barrier indeed to have stopped our men from taking their sledges to the land; and piled as the floe was against the Cape, full fifty feet high, we carried our craft over it in safety, and just in time too, for the north-west wind rushed down upon us, as if to dispute our right to intrude on its dominion. Hastily securing the tents, we hurried in to change our boots, and to see whether our feet were frost-bitten or not; for it was only by ocular proof that one could be satisfied of their safety, sensation having apparently long ceased. I shall not easily forget my painful feelings, when one gallant fellow of my party, the captain of the sledge, exclaimed, "Both feet gone, sir!" and sure enough they were, white as two lumps of ice, and equally cold; for as we of the tent party anxiously in turn placed our warm hands on the frost-bitten feet, the heat was extracted in a marvellously short time, and our half-frozen hands had to be succeeded by fresh ones as quickly as possible. With returning circulation the poor fellow's agonies must have been intense; and some hours afterwards large blisters formed over the frost-bitten parts, as if the feet had been severely scalded. Sadly cramped as we were for room, much worse was it when a sick man was amongst our number. Sleep was out of the question; and to roll up in the smallest possible compass, and try to think of something else than the cold, which pierced to the very marrow in one's bones, was our only resource.

Next day, Tuesday, 22d April, wind N. W. blowing hard, and temperature at 44° below freezing-point, parties left the encampment under Lieutenants Browne and Mecham, to look around for cairns, &c., and report upon the trend of the land, whilst the rest of us secured a dépôt of Halkett's boats, and built a cairn as a record of our visit.

As it is not my intention to give a detailed account of the operations of the Southern Division, but merely to tell of those events which will convey to the reader a general idea of the incidents connected with Arctic travelling, I shall without further comment give them, leaving to the curious in the minutiæ of the journeys the amusement of reading in the Admiralty Blue Books the details of when we eat, drank, slept, or marched.

Cape Walker was found to form the eastern and most lofty extreme of a land-trending to the south-west on its northern coast, and to the south on its eastern shore. The cape itself, full 1000 feet in altitude, was formed of red sandstone and conglomerate, very abrupt to the eastward, but dipping with an undulating outline to the west.

In its immediate neighbourhood no traces of Franklin having visited it were to be seen, and, as a broad channel ran to the southward (there was every reason to believe down to the American continent, and thence to Behring's Straits), by which Franklin might have attempted to pass, Captain Ommanney, very properly despatched Lieutenant Browne to examine the coast of Cape Walker Land, down the channel to the southward; and then, the "Success" sledge having previously departed with invalids, the five remaining sledges, on the evening of the 24th of April, marched to the westward. Previous to that date it had been impossible to move, on account of a strong gale in our faces, together with a severe temperature.

Every mile that we advanced showed us that the coast was one which could only be approachable by ships at extraordinary seasons: the ice appeared the accumulation of many years, and bore, for some forty miles, a quiet, undisturbed look. Then we passed into a region with still more aged features: there the inequalities on the surface, occasioned by the repeated snows of winter and thaws of summer, gave it the appearance of a constant succession of hill and dale. Entangled amongst it, our men laboured with untiring energy, up steep acclivities and through pigmy ravines, in which the loose snow caused them to sink deeply, and sadly increased their toil. To avoid this description of ice, amongst which a lengthened journey became perfectly hopeless, we struck in for the land, preferring the heavy snow that encumbered the beach to such a heart-breaking struggle as that on the floe. The injury had, however, been done during our last day's labour among the hummocks; a fine clear evening had given us the full effects of a powerful sunlight upon the pure virgin-snow: the painful effect, those alone can conceive who have witnessed it. All was white, brilliant, and dazzling; the eye in vain turned from earth to heaven for rest or shade,—there was none; an unclouded sunlight poured through the calm and frosty air with merciless power, and the sun, being exactly in our faces, increased the intensity of its effects.

That day several complained of a dull aching sensation in the eyeball, as if it had been overstrained, and on the morrow blindness was rapidly coming on. From experience, I can speak of the mental anxiety which must have likewise, with others, supervened, at the thought of one's entire helplessness, and the encumbrance one had become to others, who, God knows, had troubles and labour enough of their own. Gradually the film spread itself, objects became dimmer and dimmer, and at last all was darkness, with an intense horror of the slightest ray of sunlight. In this condition, many of the four sledge-parties reached a place called by us all, in commemoration of the event, "Snow-blind Point," at the entrance of a bay in 100° W. long.

Unable to advance in consequence of a severe gale, which raged for six-and-thirty hours, we found, on the 1st of May, that sixteen men and one officer were, more or less, snow-blind and otherwise unwell; a large proportion out of the entire number of thirty souls. To be ill in any place is trying enough; but such an hospital as a brown-holland tent, with the thermometer in it at 18° below zero, the snow for a bed, your very breath forming into a small snow called "barber," which penetrated into your very innermost garments, and no water to be procured to assuage the thirst of fever until snow had been melted for the purpose, called for much patience on the part of the patients, and true Samaritan feelings on the part of the "doctors,"—a duty which had now devolved on each officer of a sledge-party, or, in default of him, upon some kind volunteer amongst the men. Happily, the effects of snow-blindness are not lasting, for we recovered as suddenly as we had been struck down. The gale blew itself out, leaving all calm and still, as if the death-like scenery was incapable of such wild revelry as it had been enjoying; and again we plodded onwards, parting from the last supporting sledge on the 6th of May.

Since leaving Cape Walker on the 24th of April, we had gradually passed, in a distance of sixty miles, from a red sandstone to a limestone region; the scenery at every mile becoming more and more monotonous, and less marked by bold outline, cliff, or mountain: as far as the bay, of which Snow-blind Point formed one extreme, a long range of hills, soft and rounded in *contour*, faced the sea, and sloped to it with a gradual inclination, some three miles in length; ravines became more and more scarce; and after passing the bay, in 100° long. W., none of any size were to be seen. Drearily monotonous as all Arctic scenery must naturally be, when one universal mantle of snow makes earth and water alike, such a tame region as this was, if possible, more so; and walking along the weary terraces, which in endless succession swept far into the interior, and then only rose in diminutive heights of maybe 500 feet, I recalled to memory the like melancholy aspect of the Arctic shores of Asia as described by Baron Wrangell.

The broken and rugged nature of the floes obliged us to keep creeping along the coast-line, whilst our ignorance of the land ahead, its trend or direction, occasioned, together with the endless thick weather that we had until the 14th May, many a weary mile to be trodden over, which a knowledge of the bays or indentations would have saved us. It was under such unprofitable labour that the sterling value of our men the more conspicuously showed itself. Captain Ommanney, myself, and Mr. Webb of the "Pioneer," (who sooner than be left behind had voluntarily taken his place as one of the sledge-crew,) were the only three officers; we were consequently thrown much into the society of the men, and I feel assured I am not singular in saying that that intercourse served much to raise our opinion of the character and indomitable spirit of our seamen and marines. On them fell the hard labour, to us fell the honours of the enterprise, and to our chief the reward; yet none equalled the men in cheerfulness and sanguine hopefulness of a successful issue to our enterprise, without which, of course, energy would soon have flagged. Gallant fellows! they met our commiseration with a smile, and a vow that they could do far more. They spoke of cold as "Jack Frost," a real tangible foe, with whom they could combat and would master. Hunger was met with a laugh, and a chuckle at some future feast or jolly recollections told, in rough terms, of by-gone good cheer; and often, standing on some neighbouring pile of ice, and scanning the horizon for those we sought, have I heard a rough voice encouraging the sledge-crew by saying, "Keep step, boys! keep step! she (the sledge) is coming along almost by herself: there's the 'Erebus's' masts showing over the point ahead! Keep step, boys! keep step!"

We had our moments of pleasure too,—plenty of them, in spite of the cold, in spite of fatigue. There was an honest congratulation after a good day's work; there was the time after the pemmican had been eaten, and each one, drawing up his blanket-bag around him, sat, pannikin in hand, and received from the cook the half-gill of grog; and after drinking it, there was sometimes an hour's conversation, in which there was more hearty merriment, I trow, than in many a palace,—dry witticisms, or caustic remarks, which made one's sides-ache with laughter. An old marine, mayhap, telling a giddy lamby of a seaman to take his advice and never to be more than a simple private; for, as he philosophically argued, "whilst you're that, do you see, you have to think of nothing: there are petty officers, officers, captains, and admirals paid for looking after you and taking care of you!" or perhaps some scamp, with mock solemnity, wondering whether his mother was thinking of him, and whether she would cry if he never returned to England; on which a six-foot marine remarks, that "thank God, he has got no friends; and there would only be two people in England to cry about him,—the one, the captain of his company, who liked him because he was the tallest man in it, and the canteen sergeant, whom he had forgot to pay for some beer." Now a joke about our flags and mottoes, which one vowed to be mere jack-acting; then a learned disquisition on raising the devil, which one of the party declared he had seen done, one Sunday afternoon, for the purpose of borrowing some cash to play skittles with. In fact, care and thought were thrown to the winds; and, tired as we were, sleep often overtook us, still laughing at the men's witticisms. And then such dreams,—they seemed as if an angel had sent them to reward us for the hard realities of the day: we revelled in a sweet elysium; home was around us,—friends, kind, good friends, plenty smiled on every side; we eat, drank, and were merry; we visited old scenes with by-gone shipmates; even those who had long gone to that bourne whence traveller returneth not, came back to cheer our sleeping hours; and many a one, nigh forgot amongst the up-hill struggles of life, returned to gladden us with their smiles: and as we awoke to the morning meal, many a regret would be heard that so pleasant a delusion as the night had been spent in should be dispelled: each succeeding night, however, brought again "the cherub that watcheth over poor Jack," to throw sunny thoughts around the mind, and thus relieve our wayworn bodies.

On the 14th of May, the "Reliance" and "True Blue" sledges reached a wide break in the continuation of the land, looking like a channel, and some heights to the S. W. appeared to mark the opposite shore of a channel full twenty-five miles wide. Captain Ommanney and myself ascended an elevated mass of table-land, and looked upon the wide-spread wintry scene. Landward, to the south, and far over the rugged and frozen sea, all was death-like and silent as the grave: we felt we might have been the first since "creation's morn" to have looked upon it; the very hills were still clothed in their winter's livery, and the eye could not detect the line of demarkation between land and sea. The frozen foot-prints of a musk-ox excited our curiosity, as being the first and only ones we had seen, and, together with like traces of reindeer, a short distance from Cape Walker, was the sum total of the realization of all our once rosy anticipations of beef and venison to be found during the southern journey.

Ptarmigan, in small numbers, were occasionally seen, and about four brace shot; and now and then a stray fox was espied, watching us, although their numerous tracks showed them to be pretty plentiful: traces of hares were very numerous, but none were fallen in with by our sportsmen, except at Cape Walker, where many were seen by later visitors, and several shot; indeed, it appeared as if it was the limit, in this direction, of animal life: the Polar bears, and *ergo* the seals, not showing themselves west of the same headland in our route.

On the 17th May the "Reliance" and "True Blue" parted company, each having provisions left to enable them to advance for a further period of five days; Captain Ommanney generously allowing me, his junior, to take the search up in a westerly direction, whilst he went down the channel to the southward, which after all ended in a blind bay. I went some fifty miles farther, and, finding the coast trend to the south, endeavoured to march in a westerly direction across the floe. The sledge was light, with only ten days' provision, and the men were well inured to their work; but I saw, that from the severe strains that were brought on the fastenings of the sledge, that wood, iron, and lashings would not long stand it; and as every foot we advanced, progress became more laborious, and risk greater, I desisted in the attempt; for, situated as we were, nigh three hundred miles from our ship, the breaking down of the sledge would have entailed fearful misery, if not destruction, to my party. Turning southward, we again closed the land, when another severe storm, on the 21st of May, obliged us to take shelter in our tent, and remain there until it was time to return.

The journey homeward was light work: the sledges were now half emptied; the weather had become mild, being only a little below freezing-point; we knew the ground, and could make short cuts, and by forced marches we succeeded in making two days' journey in one, thereby giving ourselves a double quantity of food to consume. Lost flesh was quickly recovered; and the two sledges, again rejoining, reached by the night of the 4th of June a dépôt formed at Snow-blind Bay.

Here we met Lieutenant Mecham. He informed us that neither by our parties, or those of Penny's, had intelligence of Franklin been brought back by the supporting sledges. There was, however, hope yet: the long parties had not yet come in; and Captain Penny had been stopped by *water—open water*—early in May. He had again gone out with a boat; and all attention was directed to Wellington Channel, for every one felt that on no other route was there a chance of Franklin being heard of. Lastly, great fears were entertained lest our long parties should not beat those of the "Lady Franklin" and "Sophia" in time and distance; a piece of *esprit-de-corps* highly commendable, no doubt, but which, I blush to say, I took no interest in, having gone to the Arctic regions for other motives and purposes than to run races for a Newmarket cup, or to be backed against the field like a Whitechapel game-cock.

Whilst Captain Ommanney went to Cape Walker for some observations, we pulled foot (with forced marches) straight across the floe for Griffith's Island. Every hour wasted in the return journey was a crime, we felt, towards those whom we had come here to save. The fast increasing heat told that the open season was at hand: and even if we could not get our ship to the water, we had brought out a number of beautiful boats, built expressly, at a great expense; our foot journeys in the spring had been new and successful, what might we not yet expect from boat expeditions when the floes were in motion?

On reaching that part of the frozen strait which was evidently covered with only one season's ice, namely, that of about three feet in thickness, symptoms of a speedy disruption were very apparent; long narrow cracks extended continuously for miles; the snow from the surface had all melted, and, running through, served to render the ice-fields porous and spongy: the joyful signs hurried us on, though not without suffering from the lack of pure snow, with which to procure water for drinking. At last Griffith's Island rose above the horizon; a five-and-twenty-mile march brought us to it, and another heavy drag through the melting snow carried us to our ships, on the 12th June, after a journey of five hundred miles in direct lines, in fifty-eight days. We were punished for our last forced march by having five out of the sledge-crew laid up with another severe attack of snow-blindness.

Eight-and-forty hours afterwards, Captain Ommanney arrived; he had crossed some of the cracks in the floe with difficulty, aided by a bridge of boarding-pikes; and Lieut. Mecham, with the sledge "Russell," coming from Cape Walker, on the 17th of June, was obliged to desert his sledge, and wade through water and sludge to Griffith's Island, and thence to the ships: showing how remarkably the breaking up of the ice in Barrow's Strait promised to coincide in date with the time it was first seen to be in motion, by Sir E. Parry's squadron, in 1820.

All the parties were now in, except three sledges and twenty-one men, towards Melville Island; the supports in that direction had suffered in about the same ratio as ourselves to the southward; the progress, however, as might be expected where the coast-line was known, was more rapid. The total number of accidents from frost-bites amounted to eighteen, and amongst them were several cases in which portions of injured feet had to be amputated; only one man had fallen, John Malcolm, a seaman of the "Resolute;" he, poor fellow, appears to have been delicate from the outset, having fainted on his road to the place of inspection and departure, in April, 1851.

After an absence of sixty-two days, Lieut. Aldrich, with the "Lady Franklin" sledge, arrived from Byam Martin Channel. He had searched the west coast of Bathurst Island, which tended a little westerly of north until in latitude 76° 15′ N. At that point, the channel was still full twenty miles wide between Bathurst and Melville Islands, and extended northward as far as could be seen. The only things of note observed, were reindeer, in the month of *April*, on Bathurst Island, and, with the temperature at 60° below freezing-point, they were grazing on moss or lichen; this point placed beyond doubt the fact, which is now incontestable, that the animals of the Parry group do not migrate to the American continent in the winter. On his way back, Lieut. A. fell in with large flocks of wild fowl winging their way *northward*.

The floes around our ships were entirely covered with the water of the melted snow, in some places full four feet in depth, eating its way rapidly through in all directions, when Lieut. M'Clintock's sledge, the "Perseverance," and the "Resolute" sledge, Dr. Bradford's, hove in sight, having been out exactly eighty days. Lieut. M'Clintock had been to Winter Harbour, and visited all the points known to Parry's squadron, such as Bushman Cove, Cape Dundas,

&c.; but of course no traces of Franklin. He had, however, brought a portion of Parry's last wheel, used in his journey, and substantial proofs of the extraordinary abundance of animal life in that remote region, in the hides and heads of musk-oxen, the meat of which had helped to bring back his crew in wonderful condition. Eighty head of oxen and reindeer had been counted by Mr. M'Clintock, and he could have shot as many as he pleased. Dr. Bradford's journey was not so cheering a one. He had been early knocked up from a fall,—serious symptoms threatened, and for nearly a month the gallant officer was dragged upon his sledge; carrying out —thanks to his own pluck, and the zeal of his men—the object of his journey,—the search of the eastern side of Melville Island. We were now all in: Lieut. M'Clintock had fairly won the palm,—"palmam qui meruit ferat;" in eighty days he had travelled eight hundred miles, and heartily did we congratulate him on his success.

The day following, July 7th, I and one of the officers of the "Pioneer" started to visit Penny's expedition: he was expected back, and we longed to hear the news; Captain Penny having last been reported to have reached the water with a sound boat, a good crew, and a month's provisions. Landing at Cape Martyr, wet up to our necks with splashing through the pools of water, nowhere less than knee-deep, and often a mile in extent, we did not willingly leave the dry land again. On ascending a slope which gave us a view of the south shore of Cornwallis Island as far as Cape Hotham, and near a point known as that whence the dog-sledges in the winter used to strike off when communicating with the ships, our astonishment was great at finding the ice of Barrow's Strait to have broken up;—the gray light of the morning, and the perfect calm, prevented us seeing to what extent, but there was plenty of it, and a sea again gladdened our eyesight. Oh! it was a joyous, exhilarating sight, after nine months of eternal ice and snow.

The ground flew under our feet as, elevated in spirits, we walked rapidly into Assistance Bay, and grasped by the hand our old friends of the "Lady Franklin." We had each our tale to recount, our news to exchange, our hopes and disappointments to prose over. One thing was undoubtedly certain,—that, on May 16th, Captain Penny had discovered a great extent of water northward of Cornwallis Island: that this same water prevented Captain Stewart, of the "Sophia," from passing some precipitous cliffs, against which a heavy sea was beating: that this same sea was clear of all but *sea-washed* ice, and no floes were to be seen. Moreover, owing to a *southerly* breeze, which blew away to seaward the ice over which Dr. Goodsir had advanced to the westward, his retreat was nearly endangered by the water obliging him with his sledge to take to the neighbouring heights: and all this, a *month before any thing like a disruption had taken place in Barrow's Strait.* This latter event, it seems, took place about the 25th of June, 1851; and, on the 28th June, the commander of the "Sophia" had gone in a whale-boat from the entrance of the harbour to Wellington Channel.

Three days after our arrival at Assistance Harbour, not a particle of ice was to be seen, east or west, in Barrow's Strait, looking from the highland on the east side of the anchorage, except between Griffith's Island and Cape Martyr, where, some ten miles from the water, and in the centre of a fixed floe, our unlucky squadron was jammed. Every where else a clear sea spread itself, sparkling and breaking under a fresh southerly breeze. Some individuals, who had visited Cape Hotham, reported the water in Wellington Channel to have made up as high as Barlow Inlet, beyond which, up to the north water, a floe still intervened.

In default of Penny's arrival, I was much interested in a journey, upon which Mr. John Stuart, surgeon of the "Lady Franklin," had been despatched to follow the traces of some of Franklin's sledges, towards Caswell's Tower, and to re-examine the traces found in 1850. The sledge-tracts, which I have elsewhere alluded to, as existing on the east side of "Erebus and Terror Bay," Mr. Stuart found, as we conjectured, to have been those of some exploring party, sent from Beechey Island to Caswell's Tower, in Radstock Bay; for at the base of the said tower—a remarkable detached mass of limestone—two carefully-constructed cairns were found, but no record in them; beyond this, no farther signs of the missing navigators were found—nothing whatever that could indicate a retreating party. That these cairns were placed to attract attention, appears certain; the most conspicuous points have been chosen for them; they are well and carefully built, evidently not the mere work of an idle hour.

Failing Penny, and his intelligence, I contented myself with visiting the neighbourhood of Assistance Harbour, and with observing the various phenomena connected with the dissolution of the winter ice and snow upon the land; and, of these, none was more interesting than the breaking out of the ravines, which, having filled with snow during the winter, had formed, during the previous fortnight, into large lakes of water, sometimes of acres in extent; and then, in one moment, the barriers which had pent up the ravines gave way, and, with irresistible force, the waters rushed over every obstacle to the sea. Three large ravines broke open whilst I was in Assistance Harbour, and the thundering sound of the ice, water, and shingle, which swept down, and soon cut a broad channel for many yards through the floe in the bay, was a cheering tune to the gallant fellows who were looking forward to being released from their winter imprisonment.

Within twenty-four hours the body of water in these ravines would release itself, and an almost dry water-course be left. Nothing in the shape of a river seemed to exist in this island —rather a remarkable fact, considering its size, and the immense quantity of snow annually thawed in its interior valleys and plains.

A beautiful lake existed about two miles inland; and, having been discovered by one of Captain Penny's people on the anniversary of the battle of Trafalgar, was very appropriately called Trafalgar Lake; in it a small species of trout had been caught occasionally throughout the winter; and if the ice broke up early, a good haul of fish was anticipated from the seine-nets: on elevated land around the lake, sorrel and scurvy-grass grew in abundance. I need hardly say we eat of it voraciously, for the appetite delighted in any thing like vegetable food.

Occasionally eider and pin-tailed duck were shot, as well as a few brent-geese, but these birds appeared remarkably shy and wary, although evidently here to breed.

During the first week of my stay in Assistance Harbour, immense flights of wild fowl were to be seen amongst the loose ice in Barrow's Strait; but when the pack had dispersed, and left nothing but an open sea, the birds appeared to have gone elsewhere for food. Indeed, I always observed that at the edge of ice more birds were invariably to be found in the Arctic regions, than in large or open water,— a rule equally applicable to the whale, seal, and bear, all of which are to be found at the floe-edge, or in loosely-packed ice.

A gale of wind from the southward occurred, and I was extremely anxious to see whether it would bring over the ice from the opposite shore, as the croakers in Assistance Harbour, unable to deny the existence of water along the north shore of Barrow's Strait, consoled themselves by declaring that the floe had merely formed itself into pack, and was now lying along the coast of North Somerset, ready at an hour's warning to spread itself over the waters. The southerly gale, however, piped cheerily. A heavy swell and surf—Oh! most pleasant sound!—beat upon the fixed ice of Assistance Harbour; yet no pack came, nor floe-pieces either, and thus was placed beyond all doubt the fact that, at any rate, as far west as Griffith's Island, Barrow's Strait was clear of ice. In an angle formed between Leopold Island and North Somerset, there was evidently a pack; for an ice-blink, which moved daily about in that direction, showed that the mass was acted upon by the winds; and at last the southerly wind drove it up into Wellington Channel. To be condemned to inactivity, with such a body of water close at hand, was painful to all but those whose age and prudence seemed to justify in congratulating themselves on being yet frozen in; and trying as had been many disappointments we experienced in the Arctic regions, there was none that pained us more than the ill luck which had consigned our squadron, and its 180 men, to inactivity, in an icy prison under Griffith's Island, whilst so much might have been done during the thirty days that the waters of Barrow's Strait, and God only knows how much more beside, were clear from ice in every shape, and seeming to beckon us on to the north-westward.

It was now we felt the full evil result of our winter quarters. Boats could not be despatched, I suppose, because the ships might at any time in July have been swept by the ice whither it pleased, and the junction of boats and ships rendered uncertain. Future expeditions will, however, hit this nail on the head, and three distinct periods for Arctic exploration will be found to exist, viz.:—The spring, from April to June 25th, for foot journeys; from June 25th to the first week in August, for boat expeditions; and then six weeks (for steam vessels) of navigable season.

Unable to remain with satisfaction away from our squadron, to be daily tantalized with looking at a sea which might as well not have existed for us, we returned to the "Pioneer," calling the attention of the officers of Penny's squadron to the possibility of a vessel from England, sent to communicate with the squadrons, actually running past us all, and reaching Melville Island, mayhap, without detecting our winter quarters; an opinion in which all seemed to concur; and a large cairn was therefore afterwards erected upon the low land, in such a position as to attract the attention of a craft bound westward.

On our return to the Naval squadron, we found them still seven miles from the water to the southward from Griffith's Island. Towards the westward, on the 25th of July, all was water, and a water sky. About Somerville Island, and Brown Island, a patch of fixed ice, similar to that we were in, connected itself with the Cornwallis Island shore; but between that and us the water was fast making; indeed, it every day became apparent that we should be released from the *northward*, and not from the southward. One officer saw Lowther Island in a sea of water; and thus early, if not earlier, I had the firmest conviction on my mind that a ship might have been carried in a lead of water, very similar to that Parry found in 1829, into Winter Harbour, Melville Island; or, what, in view of our object, would have been more desirable, up to the north-west, by Byam Martin Channel.

Griffith's Island had, by July 25th, put on its gayest summer aspect—the ravines had emptied themselves—the snow had disappeared from the slopes—a uniform dull brown spread from one end of the island to the other—on its sheltered terraces, poppies, saxifrage, and sorrel in full flower, intermingled with lichens and mosses of every hue and description; and we, poor mortals, congratulated ourselves upon verdure, which was only charming by comparison. The great body of melted snow that had been on top of the floe, had now nearly all escaped through it in numerous fissures and holes, and they were rapidly connecting themselves one with the other. Canals, which had been formed in the floe, for the purpose of enabling the squadron to get out, should the water make exactly in the same way it did last year, now spread snake-like over the floe, and the waters of Barrow's Strait had approached to within a distance of four miles. Thus closed the month of July, with the additional disappointing intelligence, that Penny, who returned to Assistance Harbour on the 25th, had not been able, owing to the constant prevalence of contrary winds setting in from the N. W., and his want of provisions, to make much progress in Wellington Channel. Indeed, he had, from all accounts, found his boat but ill-adapted to contend with the strong breezes, heavy sea, and rapid tides into which he had launched between the islands north of Cornwallis Island, and never succeeded in obtaining a desirable offing; the islands, however, were thoroughly searched for traces; a small piece of fresh English elm was found on one of them, which Penny believed to have been thrown overboard from the "Erebus" and "Terror;" also a bit of charred pine, which Sir John Richardson believes to have been burnt by a party belonging to the same ships. But the most important result of Penny's efforts was the verification of the existence of a great body of open water, north-west, and beyond the barrier of ice which still existed in Wellington Channel.

I will not bore the reader with some days of hard labour, in which we cut to the southward into the ice, whilst the water was trying hard to get to us from the north; it eventually caught us, and (Saturday, August 8th,) we were all afloat in open water, with a barrier of ice *still southward towards Barrow's Strait.* The "Intrepid" had been sent early in the week to look round the north end of Griffith's Island, and reported a narrow neck of ice from the N. W. bluffs towards Somerville Island. Eastward, and not westward, was, however, to be our course, and we therefore remained where we were. On the 9th and 10th, a general disruption of the little remaining ice took place: we made gentle and very cautious moves towards Barrow's Strait; and, at last, on August 11th, the ice, as if heartily tired of us, shot us out into Barrow's Strait, by turning itself fairly round on a pivot. We were at sea because we could not help it, and the navigable season was proclaimed to have commenced.

Taking, like another Sinbad, our "Resolute" old burden behind us, the "Pioneer" steamed away for Assistance Harbour, from whence, as we had been given to understand some days previously, Jones's Sound was to be our destination; a plan to which I the more gladly submitted, as I felt confident, from all I had heard and seen of its geography or of that of the neighbouring land, that it would be found to connect itself with Penny's North Water: once in it we felt failure of our object to be impossible; we had still three years' provisions, and nearly four years of many things. One man had died, perhaps half-a-dozen more were invalids, but the rest were strong and hearty: to be sure, we all lacked much of that sanguineness which had animated us hitherto. Repeated disappointment, long journeys in the wrong direction (as it had proved), over regions which had, of course, shown no trace of those we had hoped to rescue—had all combined to damp our feelings.

The morning fog broke, and a day, beautiful, serene, and

sunny, welcomed us into Assistance Harbour, which we found had just cleared out of ice; and the "Lady Franklin," "Sophia," and "Felix," with anchors down, rode all ready for sea. As we towed the "Resolute" up to her anchorage, Captain Penny pulled past in his gig, evidently going to make an official visit to our leader. Directly after the "Pioneer" was secured, I went on board the "Resolute," to hear the news, her first lieutenant having been in Assistance Harbour (Captain Penny's quarters) up to the moment of our arrival. I then learned that Penny was going to volunteer to proceed up Wellington Channel, if it cleared out, in one of our steamers; and my gallant friend, the first lieutenant, spoke strongly upon the necessity of still trying to reach the North Water by the said route, whilst I maintained that, until we had visited Jones's Sound, it was impossible to say whether it would not be found an easier road into the open sea seen by Captain Penny than Wellington Channel appeared to be. Captain Penny soon joined us, and there, as well as afterwards on board the "Lady Franklin," I heard of his proposal above alluded to, which had been declined. Failing in his offer of coöperation, which was for one reason not to be wondered at,—insomuch that our large and efficient squadron needed no assistance either in men or material to do the work alone,—Captain Penny had decided on returning home, believing that Franklin was so far to the N. W. as to be beyond his reach, and also looking to the tenor of his instructions, which strictly enjoined him to return to England in 1852.

* * * * * *

Next morning, by four o'clock, we were all bound to the eastward. A few amongst those of our squadron still hoped by Jones's Sound to reach that sea of whose existence, at any rate, we had no longer any doubt, whatever might be its difficulty of access. Off Cape Hotham we found a loose pack; it extended about half way across Wellington Channel, and then a clear sea spread itself eastward and northward along the shores off North Devon to Cape Bowden. From a strong ice-blink up Wellington Channel there was reason to think the barrier* still athwart it; we did not, however, go to ascertain whether it was so, but, favoured by a fair wind, steamed, sailed, and towed the "Resolute," as fast as possible past Beechey Island. The form of sending letters to England had been duly enacted, but few were in a humour to write; the news would be unsatisfactory, and, unless Jones's Sound was an open sea, and we could not therefore help entering it, there was a moral certainty of all being in England within a short time of one another.

And so it proved. Leaving the "Assistance" and "Resolute" to join us off Cape Dudley Digges, the steamers proceeded, under Captain Austin, with three months' provisions, on the night of the 14th of August, for Jones's Sound.

Next morning brought the steamers close in with the shore between Capes Horsburgh and Osborn, along which we steered towards Jones's Sound. Glacier and iceberg again abounded, and the comparatively tame scenery of Barrow's Strait was changed for bold and picturesque mountains and

---

* Had we but happily known at that time of the perfect description of the Wellington Channel ice subsequent to our passage across in 1850, as shown by the tract of the American Expedition and Lieutenant De Haven's admirable report, we should not then have fallen into the error of believing *barriers* of ice to be permanent in deep-water channels, a fallacy which it is to be hoped has exploded with many other misconceptions as to the fixed nature of ice, and the constant accumulation of it in Polar regions.

headlands. As the evening of the 15th drew in, Jones's Sound gradually opened itself in the Coburg Bay of the charts, and, in spite of a strong head-wind, we drew up to and commenced working up it under sail and steam. During the night, Cape Leopold showed to be an island, dividing the sound into two entrances; and the exhilarating effect of a fine broad expanse of water leading to the westward, up which we were thrashing under a press of canvas, was only marred by the unpleasant fact that we had parted from the ships containing our main stock of provisions, without the means of following up any traces, should we be happy enough to discover them, of the poor missing expedition.

Saturday, August 16th, 1851.—The sound is evidently narrowest about the entrance; from a point to the N. W. of us it evidently increases in width; loose patches of ice are occasionally met with, and the tides seem somewhat strong, judging by the set of the vessel. The scenery is magnificent, especially on the south shore, where some ten miles in the interior a huge dome of pure white snow envolopes land some 3000 or 4000 feet high, which Captain Austin has named the Trenter Mountains, in compliment to the family of Sir John Barrow, (that being the maiden name of the Dowager Lady Barrow.) From this range long winding glaciers pour down the valleys, and project, through the ravines, into the deep-blue waters of this magnificent strait. Northward of us the land is peculiar, lofty table-land, having here and there a sudden dip, or thrown up in a semi-peak. The draught of the wind has blown constantly down the strait. Such are my rough notes made during the day, as the "Pioneer" and "Intrepid" worked to the westward; but as evening drew on, the increasing smoothness of the water, and a hard icy blink to the west, prepared us for a report which came from the crow's nest about midnight, that there was very much ice to the windward of us.

Next day, 17th, after a fog which caused some delay had cleared off, the disagreeable truth revealed itself: from a little beyond a conical-shaped island on the north shore, the sound was still barred with floes, although at this point it increased at least twelve miles more in breadth. Going up to the floe-edge, the steamers crossed to the S. W., following the ice carefully along until it impinged upon the southern shore. The night was beautifully serene and clear; and, as if to add to our regret, four points and a half of the compass, or 54° of bearing to the westward, showed no symptom of land. The northern side of the sound trended away to the west, preserving its lofty and marked character; whilst on the south the land ended abruptly some fifteen miles farther on, and then, beyond a small break, one of those wedge-shaped hills peculiar to the limestone lands of Barrow's Strait showed itself at a great distance; and the natural suggestion to my own mind was, that the opening between the said wedge-shaped hill and the land on our southern hand would have been found to connect itself with the deep fiords running to the northward from Croker Bay, in Lancaster Sound; and for an opinion as to the direction of Jones's Sound, whose frozen surface forbade us to advance with our vessels, I was, from what I saw, fully willing to believe in the report of my ice quarter-master, Robert Moore, a clever, observant seaman, as the annexed report will show:—

"SIR,

"It was in 1848 that I was with Captain Lee in the 'Prince of Wales,' when we ran up Jones's Sound. The wind was from the S. S. E. compass (*E. N. E. true*), thick weather, with a strong breeze. We steered up Jones's

Sound, N. E. by compass (*westwardly true*), for fourteen hours, when, seeing some ice aground, we hauled to.

"The next day, being fine weather, we proceeded farther up, and seeing no ice or fish (*whales*), a boat was sent on shore. She, returning, reported not having seen any thing but *very high land* and *deep water close to* rocks on the south shore.

"We tacked ship, and stood to the N. E. compass (*N. W. true*); saw some ice aground on a sand-bank, with only six feet water on it at low water, but standing on the N. E. compass (*N. W. true*), found deep water from five to eight miles across from the sand to the north shore. When past the sand, open water as far as we could see from the mast-head, and extending from about *N. E. to N. N. W. compass* (N. W. to W. S. W. true). We then returned, being fine and clear, and could not see what we were in search of (whales).

"Leaving the north land, a long, low point, running up to a *table-top mountain, we came across to the south side, which was bold land right out of the sound.*

"We saw the *Pinnacle Rocks at the end of that sound* (*Princess Charlotte's Monument*); and *this and the low land between that sound* and *Lancaster Sound*, as we were running to the S. E., makes me confident is the same place which we were up in the 'Pioneer.'

"The distance we ran up the sound in the 'Prince of Wales,' I think, to the best of my judgment, was about a hundred and fifty or sixty miles, &c.

"(Signed) ROBERT MOORE,
"Ice quarter-master, H. M. S. 'Pioneer.'

"To Lieut. Sherard Osborn."

The italics in the above letter serve to show how correctly these observations of my quarter-master agreed with the sound we were up; and taking this, together with the description of the land seen by Captain Stewart and Dr. Sutherland, during their late journey up the eastern side of Wellington Channel, I believe that a very narrow intervening belt of low land divides Jones's Sound from Baring Bay, in Wellington Channel, and that, turning to the northward, this sound eventually opens into the same great Polar Sea which washes the northern shores of the Parry group.

Unable to advance, we returned, upon our wake, to the conical island on the north side of the sound; and a boat, with two officers in it, was sent to erect a cairn. They returned next morning, having found, what interested me very much, numerous Esquimaux traces, though of very ancient date, and shot several birds—a seasonable increase to our stock for table-consumption. One of the sportsmen assured me that, in spite of the increased number of glaciers around us, and other appearances of a more severe climate than we had been in the habit of seeing in Barrow's Strait, he was of opinion that there was much more vegetation in our neighbourhood than in the more southern latitude of Cornwallis Island. The specimens of plants brought off in the boat, such as poppies, saxifrage, and moss, were all finer than we had seen elsewhere; and reindeer horns, near the Esquimaux ruins, showed that these animals were to be found.

The island was a mass of gray-coloured granite, with some dark masses of ferruginous-coloured rock intermixed, the whole much broken and rent by the agency of frost and water.

Monday, the 18th of August, we proceeded along the northern shore, towards another entrance which had shown itself on the north side of Leopold Island,—the Jones's Sound of the old charts,—which we now proved not to have been blocked up by either land or glaciers.

The land about Cape Hardwicke was little else, in my opinion, than a group of islands,—an impression in which I became the more confirmed when the ice obliged us to strike off directly to the eastward; and Cape Clarence stood out bold and clear, with a midnight sun behind it: and the light streamed through the different ice-choked channels between Capes Hardwicke and Clarence, throwing up the land, *where there was land*, in strong and dark relief.

Beyond Cape Clarence I saw no symptom of land, nor did any one else either. It is said to recede; very possibly it may; but as neither we, nor the "Resolute" and "Assistance," (who all reached a higher latitude than any discovery-ships have been since Baffin's memorable voyage,) ever saw land north of Cape Clarence, I trust, for the sake of geography, that the beautifully-indented line which now joins the land about Smith's Sound to that of Clarence Head, in our charts, may be altered into a dotted one, as denoting that the said coast exists rather in the imagination of channel-closing voyagers than actually in the north-west corner of Baffin's Bay.

A multitude of grounded icebergs showed a shoal, which appears to bar the northern entrance to Jones's Sound; and, during the night, a sudden gale from the north, together with high water in the tides, set them all floating and dancing around us in a very exciting style. Edging constantly along large floe-pieces, we were eventually carried next day into the packed ice, through which our way had to be found under double-reefed sails, the two pretty screw-schooners thrashing away in gallant style, until a dead calm again left us to steam our best; indeed, all night of the 19th was a constant heavy tussle with a pack, in which the old floe-pieces were being glued together by young ice, varying from two to five inches in thickness; patches of water, perhaps each an acre in extent, were to be seen from the crow's nest, and from one to the other of these we had to work our way. By-and-by the Cary Isles showed themselves to the northward, and then the flat-topped land between Cape York and Dudley Digges.

Our last hope of doing any service this season lay in the expectation that open water would be found along the north-east side of Baffin's Bay; but this expectation was damped by the disagreeable knowledge that our provisions on board the steamers were too scanty to allow us to follow up any opening we should have found.

On the afternoon of the 28th of August, a strong water-sky and heavy bank showed the sea to be close at hand to the south, as well as a strong breeze behind it. We rattled on for Wolstenholme Island, reached under its lee by the evening, and edged away to the north, quickly opening out Cape Stair, and finding it to be an island, as the Cape York Esquimaux, on board the "Assistance," had led us to believe. Passing some striking-looking land, which, although like that of the more southern parts of Greenland, was bold and precipitous, intersected with deep valleys, yet comparatively free from glaciers, we saw the Booth Sound of Sir John Ross, and shortly afterwards sighted what proved afterwards to be the southern bluff of Whale Sound. We could not approach it, however, and, choosing an iceberg, we anchored our steamers to await an opening.

On Thursday, the 21st of August, I started in a boat with Mr. MacDougal, to see if we could get as far as Whale Sound. The bay-ice, in which we could neither pull nor sail, whilst it was too thin to stand upon, or track the boat through, materially checked our progress. By the afternoon we reached a close pack-edge, which defied farther progress; but, on landing, we found ourselves to be at the entrance of a magnificent inlet, still filled with ice, which extended to the eastward for some fifteen miles, having in its centre a peculiarly-shaped rock, which the seamen immediately christened "Prince Albert's Hat," from its resemblance to a marine's shako. The numerous traces here of Esquimaux were perfectly startling; their tent-places, winter abodes, cachés, and graves, covered every prominent point about us. Of what date they were, it was impossible, as I have elsewhere said, to form a correct idea. The enamel was still perfect on the bones of the seals which strewed the rocks, the flesh of which had been used for food. On opening one of the graves, I found the skeleton of an old man, with a good deal of the cartilage adhering to the bones, and in the skull there was still symptoms of decaying flesh; nothing, however, was seen to denote a recent visit of these interesting denizens of the north. Each caché, or rather, circle of stones, had a flat slab for a cover, with a cairn near it, or else an upright mass of stone, to denote its position; and some of the graves were constructed with a degree of care and labour worthy of a more civilized people: several had huge slabs of stone on the top, which it must have required a great many men to lift, and some ingenuity to secure.

Scurvy-grass in great abundance, as well as another antiscorbutic plant, bearing a small white flower, was found wherever we landed; and I likewise observed London-pride, poppies, sorrel, dwarf willow, crow-feet grass, saxifrage, and tripe-de-roche, besides plenty of turf, which, with very little trouble, would have served for fuel,—and this in latitude 76° 52′ N. Large flocks of geese and ducks were flying about; the great northern diver passed overhead, and uttered its shrill warning cry to its mate, and loons, dovekies, and plalaropes, in small numbers, gave occasional exercise for our guns.

The coast was all of granitic formation: and if one might judge from the specimens of iron pyrites and copper ore found here and there, the existence of minerals in large quantities, as is the case about Uppernavik, may be taken for granted.

The 22d, 23d, 24th, and 25th of August passed without a favourable change taking place; indeed, by this time our retreat, as well as advance, had been barred by the pack. Pressed up from Baffin's Bay by the southerly gales of this season of the year, the broken floes seemed to have been seeking an outlet by the north-west. The winter was fast setting in, temperature falling thus early, and the birds every day more scarce.

About one o'clock on the morning of the 26th August, I was aroused and told that Esquimaux were coming off on dog-sledges. All hands turned out voluntarily to witness the arrival of our visitors. They were five in number, each man having a single sledge. As they approached, they uttered an expression very like Tima! or rather Timouh! accompanied by a loud, hoarse laugh. Some of our crew answered them, and then they appeared delighted, laughing most immoderately.

The sledges were entirely constructed of bone, and were small, neat-looking vehicles: no sledge had more than five dogs; some had only three. The dogs were fine-looking, wolfish animals, and either white or tan colour. The well-fed appearance of the natives astonished us all; without being tall (averaging about 5 ft. 5 in.), they were brawny-looking fellows, deep-chested, and large-limbed, with Tartar beards and moustachios, and a breadth of shoulder which denoted more than ordinary strength. Their clothing consisted of a dressed seal-skin frock, with a hood which served for a cap when it was too cold to trust to a thick head of jet-black hair for warmth. A pair of bear-skin trowsers reaching to the knee, and walrus-hide boots, completed their attire. Knowing how perfectly isolated these people were from the rest of the world,—indeed, they are said with some degree of probability to have believed themselves to be the only people in the world,—I was not a little delighted to see how well necessity had taught them to clothe themselves; and the skill of the women was apparent in the sewing, and in one case tasteful ornamental work of their habiliments.

I need hardly say that we loaded them with presents: their ecstacy exceeded all bounds when each was presented with a boat-hook staff, a piece of wood some twelve feet long. They danced, shouted, and laughed again with astonishment at possessing such a prize. Wood was evidently with them a scarce article; they had it not even to construct sledges with. York, the interpreter, had before told us they had no canoes for want of it; and they seemed perfectly incapable of understanding that our ships and masts were altogether made of wood. The intelligence shown by these people was very gratifying; and from having evidently been kindly treated on board the "North Star," during her sojourn in this neighbourhood, they were confident of good treatment, and went about fearlessly. On seeing a gun, they laughed, and said, "Pooh! pooh!" to imitate its sound. One man danced, and was evidently anxious to repeat some nautical shuffling of the feet to the time of a fiddle, of which he had agreeable recollections, whilst another described how we slept in hammocks. After some time, a document was given them, to show any ship they might visit hereafter; and they were sent away in high spirits. The course they had taken, both coming and going, proved them to be from Wolstenholme

Sound; and, as well as we could understand, they had lately been to the northward, looking for pousies (seals), and no doubt were the natives whose recent traces had been seen by some of the officers near Booth Inlet, who had likewise observed the remnants of some old oil-cask staves, which once had been in an English whaler.

August 26th, 1851.—Beset against a floe, which is in motion, owing to the pressure of bergs upon its southern face; and as it slowly *coachwheels* (as the whalers term it) round upon an iceberg to seaward of us, we employ ourselves heaving clear of the danger. A gale fast rising, and things looking very ugly. The "Intrepid," who had changed her berth from the "inshore" to the "offshore" side of the "Pioneer," through some accident of ice-anchors slipping, was caught between the floe and the iceberg, and in a minute inextricably, as far as human power was concerned, surrounded with ice; and as the floe, acted upon by the pressure of bergs and ice driving before the gale, forced more and more upon the berg, we were glad to see the vessel rise up the inclined plane formed by the tongue of the iceberg under her bottom. Had she not done so, she must have sunk. Sending a portion of our crew to keep launching her boats ahead during the night, we watched with anxiety the fast-moving floes and icebergs around us. A wilder scene than that of this night and the next morning it would be impossible to conceive. Our forced inactivity—for escape or reciprocal help was impossible—rendered it the more trying.

Lieutenant Cator has himself told the trials to which the "Intrepid's" qualities were subjected that night and day; how she was pushed up the iceberg high and dry; and how the bonnie screw came down again right and tight. We meanwhile drifted away, cradled in floe-pieces, and perfectly helpless, shaving past icebergs, in close proximity, but safely, until the gale as suddenly abated, and we found ourselves some six miles north of the "Intrepid," and off the Sound, which, for want of a name, we will call "Hat Sound." Steaming and sailing up a head of water back towards our consort, we soon saw that she was all right and afloat again, though beset in the pack. We therefore took advantage of an opening in the ice to run to the northward alone. About midnight, the Whale Sound of Baffin being then open to our view, but filled with broken ice, and our farther progress impeded by the pack, we again made fast at this, the farthest northern latitude reached by any of our squadron, viz., 77° north latitude.

Friday, August 29th.—Finding progress in this direction hopeless, we rejoined the "Intrepid" as close as the ice would allow us, and learnt that she had injured her rudder and screw-framing. It was now decided to rejoin the "Resolute" and "Assistance" at their rendezvous off Cape Dudley Digges; and as the winter snow was fast covering the land, and pancake-ice forming on the sea, there was little time to be lost in doing so.

The 30th and 31st, the "Pioneer" made fruitless attempts to reach the "Intrepid." The leads of water were evidently separating us more and more: she was working in for Wolstenholme Sound, whilst we were obliged to edge to the westward.

September 1st, 1851, came in on us. From the crow's nest one interminable barrier of ice spread itself around; and as the imprisonment of our vessels would have entailed starvation upon us, it was necessary to make a push, and endeavour, by one of us at any rate reaching supplies, to secure the means of rescue to both.

A lucky slackening of the ice encouraged us to enter the pack, and we entered it. It was a long and tough struggle, sometimes for an hour not making a ship's length of headway, then bursting into a crack of water, which seemed an ocean by comparison. Screwing and heaving, my gallant crew working like Britons, now over the stern, booming off pieces from the screw as she went astern for a fresh rush at some obstinate bar; now over the bows, coaxing her sharp stem into the crack which had to be wedged open until the hull could pass; now leaping from piece to piece of the broken ice, clearing the lines, resetting the anchors, then rushing for the ladders, as the vessel cleared the obstacles, to prevent being left behind,—light-hearted, obedient, and zealous, if my heartfelt admiration of them could have lightened their labours, I should have been glad indeed. Late in the evening, the "Intrepid" was seen working inside of Wolstenholme Island: we made fast to a lofty iceberg, to obtain a good view, for the most promising lead of water; and the experienced eye of a quarter-master, Joseph Organ, enabled him to detect the glisten of open water on the horizon to the westward. For it we accordingly struck through the pack. Never were screw and steam more taxed. To stop was to be beset for the winter, and be starved and drifted Heaven knows where. An iron stem and a good engine did the work,—I will not bore the non-professional reader how. A little before midnight the "Resolute" and "Assistance" were seen, and by four o'clock on the morning of the 2d September we were alongside of them. Shortly afterwards our amateurs and visitors left us, and the three vessels cruised about, waiting for the "Intrepid," it being generally understood that when she rejoined the squadron we were to return to England.

We learned that the ships had been in open water as high

as the Cary Islands: *they had seen no land on the west side, north of Cape Clarence.* On Cary Islands they had found traces of the remote visits of whalers, and had shot immense numbers (about 700) of birds, loons especially. On one occasion they had been placed in trying circumstances by a gale from the southward amongst the packed ice, the extraordinary disappearance of which to the northward, was only to be accounted for by supposing the ice of Baffin's Bay to have been blown through Smith's Sound into the Polar Sea, a small gateway for so much ice to escape by. In my opinion, however, the disappearance of the ice, which a fortnight earlier had spread over the whole sea between the Arctic Highlands and Jones's Sound, under the influence of southerly gales, confirmed me the more strongly in my belief that the north-west portion of Baffin's Bay is open, and forms no *cul-de-sac* there any more than it does in Jones's Sound, Lancaster Sound, or Pond's Bay.

From Hudson's Straits, in latitude 60° N., to Jones's Sound, in latitude 76° N., a distance of 960 miles, we find on the western hand a mass of islands, of every conceivable shape and size, with long and tortuous channels intersecting the land in every direction; yet vain men, anxious to put barriers in the way of future navigators, draw large continents, where no one has dared to penetrate to see whether there be such or not, and block up natural outlets without cause or reason.

I will now, with the reader's permission, carry him back to a subject that here and there has been cursorily alluded to throughout these pages—the Esquimaux traces and ruins, every where found by us, and the extraordinary chain of evidence which, commencing in Melville Island, our farthest west, carries us, link by link, to the isolated inhabitants of North Greenland, yclept Arctic Highlands.

Strange and ancient signs were found by us in almost every sheltered nook on the seaboard of this sad and solitary land,—signs indubitably of a race having once existed, who have either decayed away, or else, more probably, migrated to more hospitable portions of the Arctic zone. That all these traces were those of the houses, cachés, hunting-posts, and graves of the Esquimaux, or Innuit, there could be on our minds no doubt; and looking to the immense extent of land over which this extraordinary race of fishermen have been, and are to be found, well might Captain Washington, the talented compiler of the Esquimaux vocabulary, say, that they are one "of the most widely-spread nations of the globe."

The seat of this race (arguing from traditions extant during Baron Wrangell's travels in Siberia) might be placed in the north-east extreme of Asia, the western boundary being ill defined; for on the dreary banks of the Lena and Indigirka, along the whole extent of the frozen *Tundra*, which faces the Polar Sea, and in the distant isles of New Siberia, rarely visited by even the bold seekers of fossil ivory, the same ruined circles of stone, betokening the former abode of human beings, the same whalebone rafters, the same stone axes, the same implements of the chase, are to be found as to this day are used, and only used, by the Tchuktches of Behring's Straits, the Innuit of North America, or the Esquimaux of Hudson's Straits and Greenland,—a people identical in language (of which they all speak different dialects), habits, and disposition.

Supposing, then, that from the east of Asia these people first migrated to the American continent, and thence, eventually wandered to the eastern shores of Greenland, it became an interesting question to us, how the lands upon our northern hand, in our passage to the west up Barrow's Strait, should bear such numerous marks of human location, whereas upon the southern side they were comparatively scarce; and how the natives residing in the northern portion of Baffin's Bay should have been ignorant that their brethren dwelt in great numbers southward of the glaciers of Melville Bay.

Some amongst us—and I was of this number—objected to the theory summarily advanced, that at a remote period these northern lands had been peopled from the south, and that the population had perished or wasted away from increased severity of climate or diminution of the means of subsistence. Our objections were argued on the following grounds:—If the Parry group had been colonized from the American continent, that continent, their nursery, would have shown signs of a large population at points immediately in juxtaposition, which it does not do.

From the estuary of the Coppermine to the Great Fish River, the Esquimaux traces are less numerous than on the north shore of Barrow's Strait. To assert that the Esquimaux have travelled from the American continent to the bleak shores of Bathurst Island, is to suppose a savage capable of voluntarily quitting a land of plenty for one of gaunt famine: on the other hand, it seems unreasonable to attribute these signs of a by-gone people's existence to some convulsion of nature, or some awful increase of cold, since no similar catastrophe has occurred in any other part of the world. Contrary to such opinions, we opined that the traces were those of a vast and prolonged emigration, and that it could be shown, on very fair premises, that a large number of the Innuit, Skræling, or Esquimaux—call them what you please—had travelled from Asia to the eastward along a much higher parallel of latitude than the American continent, and, in their very natural search for the most hospitable region, had gone from the *north towards the south*, *not from the south towards the north*, or, what may yet one day be laid open to the world, reached a high northern latitude, in which a deep and uncongealable sea gives rise to a milder climate and an increased amount of the capabilities of subsistence.

I will now lightly sketch the probable route of the Esquimaux emigration, as I believe it to have taken place in the north-east of Asia. The Tchuktches, the only independent tribe in Siberia, are seen to assume, amongst that portion of them residing on the sea-coast, habits closely analogous to those of the Esquimaux. The hunters of Siberia tell how a similar race, the Omoki, "whose hearths were once more numerous on the banks of the Lena than the stars of an Arctic night," are gone, none know whither. The natives now living in the neighbourhood of Cape Chelajskoi, in Siberia, aver that emigration to a land in the *north-east* had occurred within the memory of their fathers; and amongst other cases we find them telling Wrangell, that the Onkillon tribe had once occupied that land, but, being attacked by the Tchuktches, they, headed by a chief called Krachnoi, had taken shelter in the land visible northward from Cape Jakan.

This land, Wrangell and others did not then believe in. British seamen have, however, proved the assertion to be a fact; and Captains Kellett and Moore have found "an extensive land" in the very direction the Siberian fishermen declared it to exist. It is not my purpose to enter into a disquisition upon the causes which brought about this emigration. Sad and bitter necessity alone it must have been which thrust these poor members of the human family into localities which, even in Asia, caused the Russians to exclaim, "What could have led men to forsake more favoured lands for this grave of Nature?" Choice it could not have been, for, in America, we see that the Esquimaux has struggled hard to reach southern and genial climes. In the Aleutian Isles, and on the coast of Labrador, local circumstances favoured the attempt, and the Indian hunter was unable to subsist in lands which were, comparatively, overflowing with subsistence for the Arctic fishermen; but elsewhere the bloodthirsty races of North America obliged the human tide, which for some wise cause was made to roll along the margin of the Polar Sea, to confine itself purely to the sea-coast; and although vast tracts, such as the barren grounds between longitudes 99° and 109° W., are at the present day almost untenanted, still a sufficient population remains to show that an emigration of these tribes had taken place there at a remote period.

These people reached, in time, the shores of Davis's Straits and the Atlantic Ocean; and, in a line parallel to them, others of their brethren who reached the land lately re-discovered, northward of Behring's Straits, may have likewise wandered along the Parry Group to Lancaster Sound.

In order to have done this, land must be presumed to extend from the meridian of Behring's Straits to Melville Island,—a point upon which few who study the geography of that region can have now a doubt; and eminent men have long supposed it to be the case,* from various phenomena, such as the shallow nature of the sea between the Mackenzie River and Behring's Straits, and the non-appearance of heavy ice in that direction—all indicating that a barrier lay northward of the American continent. The gallant squadron, under Captains Collinson and M'Clure, will, doubtless, solve this problem, and connect, either by a continent or a chain of islands, the ruined *yourts* of Cape Jakan with the time-worn stone huts of Melville Island.

---

* The present talented hydrographer of the navy, Sir F. Beaufort, foretold to the author, a year before it was discovered, the existence of land north of Behring's Straits.

Situated as these places are, under the same degree of latitude, the savage, guided by the length of his seasons and the periodical arrival of bird and beast, would fearlessly progress along the north shore of the great strait, which may be said to extend from Lancaster Sound to the Straits of Behring. This progress was, doubtless, a work of centuries, but gradual, constant, and imperative. The seal, the reindeer, and the whale, all desert or avoid places where man or beast wages war on them whilst multiplying their species, and have to be followed, as we find to be the case with our hunters, sealers, and whalers of the present day.

As the northern Esquimaux travelled to the east, offshoots from the main body no doubt struck to the southward. For instance, there is every reason to believe Boothia to have been originally peopled from the north. The natives seen there by Sir John Ross spoke of their fathers having fished and lived in more northern lands. They described the shores of North Somerset sufficiently to show that they knew that it was only by rounding Cape Bunny, that Ross could carry his vessel into that western sea, from whose waters an isthmus barred him: and this knowledge, traditional as I believe it to have been, has since been proved to be correct by those who wintered in Leopold Harbour finding Esquimaux traces about that neighbourhood, and by the foot journey of Sir James Ross, in 1848, round Cape Bunny towards the Magnetic Pole.

In corroboration of my idea that these inhabitants of the Arctic zone were once very numerous along the north shore of Barrow's Strait and Lancaster Sound, the following localities were found to abound with ruins:—The gulf between Bathurst and Cornwallis Land, the whole southern shore of Cornwallis Island, Wellington Channel, Cape Spenser, and Cape Riley; Radstock Bay, Ommanney Harbour, near Cape

Warrender, where the "Intrepid" discovered numerous well-finished graves, bearing the marks of a *comparatively* more recent date. Passing Cape Warrender, I supposed the remnant of the northern emigration from Asia to have still travelled round the coast; the more so, as at Jones's Sound, the only spot one of our officers happened to land upon, Esquimaux had evidently once lived. (*Vide* page 173.) The Arctic Highlander, Erasmus York, who was serving in our squadron, seemed to believe his mother to have dwelt about Smith's Sound: all his ideas of things that he had heard of, but not seen, referred to places northward. He knew a musk-ox when shown a sketch of one, and said that they were spoken of by his brethren: with a pencil he could sketch the coast-line *northward* of where he embarked, Cape York, as far as Whale Sound, or even farther, by tradition; but *southward* he knew of nothing.

Old whale-fishermen say that, when in former days their pursuit carried them into the head of Baffin's Bay, they found the natives numerous; and it is undoubted that, in spite of an apparently severe mortality amongst these Arctic Highlanders, or Northern Esquimaux, the stock is not yet extinct. Every whaler who has visited the coast northward of Cape York, during late years, reports deserted villages and dead bodies, as if some sudden epidemic had cut down men and women suddenly and in their prime. Our squadron found the same thing. The "Intrepid's" people found in the huts of the natives which were situated close to the winter quarters of the "North Star," in Wolstenholme Sound, numerous corpses, unburied, indeed, as if the poor creatures had been suddenly cut off, and their brethren had fled from them. Poor York, who, amongst the dead, recognized his own brother, described the malady of which they died as one of the chest or lungs: at any rate, the mortality was great.

Where did the supply of human life come from? Not from the south, for then the Northern and Southern Esquimaux would have known of each other's existence. Yet the Southern Esquimaux have faint traditions of the head of Baffin's Bay and Lancaster Sound; and Egede and Crantz tell us of their belief in a northern origin, and of their tales of remote regions where beacons on hills had been erected to denote the way. Surely all this points to the long and landward route pursued by this extraordinary people.

It may be quite possible that a portion of the Esquimaux crossed Davis's Straits by accident from the west to the east: such things have occurred within the memory of living men; but I deny that it would ever be a voluntary act, and therefore unlikely to have led to the population of South Greenland. A single hunter of seals, or more, might have been caught in the ice and been drifted across, or a boat's load of women may have been similarly obliged to perform a voyage which would have been very distasteful to an Esquimaux; but such accidents do not populate countries.

Lastly, before I quit this subject, it would be as well to call the attention of those interested in such questions to the extraordinary fact of the existence of a constantly starving race upon the *east* side of Greenland. The Danish surveyor's (Capt. Graah) remarks lead me to the opinion that these people come from more northern parts of their own side of Greenland; and it would be a curious circumstance if future geographical discoveries should give us grounds to believe that from the neighbourhood of Smith's Sound the Esquimaux migration divided, and the one branch of it followed down the shores of Baffin's Bay and Davis's Straits, whilst the other, tracing the northern coasts of Greenland, eventually descended by the eastern seaboard to Cape Farewell. The nursery, the hot-bed of this race, I believe to exist northward of spots visited by us in Baffin's Strait,—for bay it is not, even if it had no other outlets into the Polar Sea than Lancaster, Jones's, and Smith's Sound.

Revenons à nos moutons! The 2d, 3d, and 4th of September passed with much anxiety; the signals thrown out by our leader, "Where do you think the 'Intrepid' is gone?" and on another occasion, "Do you think the 'Intrepid' is to leeward of the pack?" denoting how much he was thinking of the missing steamer. We of the sister screw had little anxiety as to her safety or capability of escaping through any pack; especially when alone and unhampered by having to keep company. A knowledge of the screw, its power, and handiness, gave us a confidence in it, which we had never reason to regret. At first we had been pitied, as men doomed to be cast away: we had since learned to pity others, and to be envied in our safe vessels. The "great experiment," as it was called, had succeeded, in spite of the forebodings of the ignorant and the half-measured doubts of questionable friends; but its crowning triumph was yet to come: the *single steamer* was, alone, unaided, to penetrate the pack and seek her missing mate. Find her, if she could; if not, winter, and seek with foot parties, both this autumn and next spring.

There was a momentary pang of regret on the morning of the 5th September, when I first learned that the "Pioneer" was to return into Wolstenholme Sound with provisions sufficient for herself and the "Intrepid" to meet *two* winters more; but pride soon, both with myself and my officers and men, came to the rescue. The "Intrepid" might have been caught, and unable to extricate herself. Of course it was an honourable mission to go to the aid of our comrades, to give them the means of subsistence, to spend the winter with them, and, please God, escape next season, if not before, from the disagreeable position into which our summer tour in

Baffin's Bay had carried us: and furthermore, the screws, helpless babes! were to winter alone, alone to find their way in and out of the ice, and alone make their way home, whilst the huge incubi that had ridden us like nightmares during the search for Franklin would be (D. V.) safely lashed in Woolwich dockyard.

The 5th was spent in sending away all our sickly or weak hands, increasing the complement of seamen by four, receiving abundance of public and private stores, bidding good-bye to our dear brother officers in the squadron, and friends, who generously pressed upon us every thing they had to spare, in which they were not more generous than our leader, who put, with the utmost liberality, both his kit and storeroom at our disposal. The "Pioneer" was by midnight as deep as a sand-barge. Next morning the commodore came on board, gave me highly flattering orders, and, having read prayers, made a speech, in which he took an affectionate farewell of the "Pioneers," and struck with happy effect the two strongest chords in our hearts, thus:—"You hold," said he, "Pioneers, the honour of the squadron in your hands. I thank you all for the alacrity and spirit with which you have prepared yourselves to re-enter the ice. You shall be no losers by it; and on my arrival in England I will take care to insure that you are not forgotten in rewards: indeed, I shall consider that you have the first claim, provided your commander, on his arrival in England, reports favourably on your conduct." At eight o'clock we parted company, and, under sail and steam, steered direct for Wolstenholme Island.

A little after ten o'clock we broke through a neck of ice, and had just put the helm up to run down a lead, when, happening to look over my shoulder at the "Resolute," now hull down to the westward, I was astonished to see what appeared the smoke of a gun, and soon afterwards another, and another. The general recall at the mast-head was next seen, and the "Assistance," under all sail, pressing to the south, showed that the "Intrepid" had been caught sight of. Joy was strongly marked on every countenance as we turned on our heel, and one exclamation—"Thank God for our escape from a second winter," was on every tongue. It would have been indeed an unprofitable detention to have been caught in Wolstenholme Sound by the pack, as we undoubtedly should have been, whilst the vessel we went to relieve was safe without it. However, the evil was now averted; the whole squadron was united, my provisions, men, and stores again taken out, and a memorandum issued, the purport of which was that we were to go to Woolwich. At eight o'clock the yards were squared, sails spread, and homeward we steered.

Fresh and fair gales, a sea entirely clear of all but stray icebergs, and here and there a patch of broken ice, gave us nothing to do but endeavour to reduce our speed sufficiently under canvas to insure not outrunning our consorts. In eight days we reached the latitude of Cape Farewell. Once in the Atlantic, strong gales and dark nights rendered it impossible for such ill-matched consorts to keep company, and we found ourselves alone, sighting the Orkneys fourteen days after bearing up from the latitude of Wolstenholme Island in Baffin's Bay, and anchored at Grimsby in the river Humber, exactly three weeks from the commencement of our homeward-bound voyage. The rest of the squadron followed us to Woolwich, where all were paid off safe and sound, with the exception of one man, the only one missing out of the original one hundred and eighty officers and men who had sailed in 1850, under Captain Horatio T. Austin, C. B., to rescue or solve the fate of the expedition commanded by Captain Sir John Franklin.

Our self-importance as Arctic heroes of the first water received a sad downfall when we were first asked by a kind friend, what the deuce we came home for? We had a good many *becauses* ready, but he overturned them altogether; so we had resort to the usual resource of men in such a position: we said, "There was a barrier of ice across Wellington Channel in 1850." Our friend said, "I deny it was a permanent one, for the Americans drifted through it!" "Indeed!" we exclaimed, "at any rate there was one there in 1851." "Yes, granted, on the 12th of August; but you know there was a month of open season left: and, like an honest man, say how long it would take for that barrier, fifteen or twenty miles wide, to disperse." "As many hours!" was our reply: "and we have forsworn in future barriers of ice as well as barriers of land."

What the deuce we came home for? and why we deserted Franklin? were pleasant questions; and at first we felt inclined to be angry. Those, however, who asked them had cause and reason for doing so. We were in the dark as to much that had been arrived at in England. We knew but of our own limited personal experience, and had had neither time nor opportunity to compare notes with others. The public at home sat down with the accumulated evidence of two British expeditions and an American one. They passed a verdict that Franklin had gone up Wellington Channel, and that, having gone up there, in obedience to his country's orders, it was the duty of that country to send after him, save him, or solve his fate. I for one knew I had done my duty in the sphere allotted to me, although feeling at first that the public verdict reflected somewhat upon me as well as others. But "Vox populi, vox Dei." I bowed tacitly to its decision, until attempts were made to damp the hopes of the more sanguine,—in fact, to save our credit at the expense of Franklin's existence. It was time then to reconsider in all its points the subject of farther search, to compare my own recent impression of things with facts that were now before the world, and then to judge for myself whether any one had a right to declaim against farther efforts to save Franklin's expedition.

Need I say I found none. On comparing the information, the phenomena observed in our own squadron with those of Captain Penny's, and the Americans under Lieutenant De Haven, I saw more and more clearly that a northern sea, an open water, must have been close to us in 1850 and 1851, when we were about Wellington Channel; that that sea was *not* blocked with ice in 1850, as we had ignorantly supposed; and that as assuredly as it was proved that Sir John Franklin had not gone to Cape Walker, nor disobeyed his orders by going to Melville Island, so certain did it now become that up Wellington Channel he had steered to that open sea, which, whether limited or encircling the Pole, it was his object to enter. It was water and an open sea that Franklin wanted to achieve the North-west Passage; and there it was before him. Can any one suppose him, accuse him, capable of hesitating to enter it?

Those who will not admit this, have recourse to two infallible Arctic solutions for the dilemma in which they are placed; it must be either an impenetrable barrier of ice in Wellington Channel, or the ships must have been beset in the pack, and have perished, without God's providence helping them, as it has helped all others similarly placed, without leaving a single survivor or a vestige of any description. No such wholesale calamity is on record.

Let us inquire into this barrier of ice in Wellington Channel. Twice had Parry seen the channel, in 1819 and 1820; he saw no barrier then. We reached it in the fall of 1850, after a very backward and severe summer, with winter fast closing in upon us. We saw long flights of birds retreating from their summer breeding-places somewhere beyond the broad fields of ice that lay athwart its channel. We wondered at the numerous shoals of white whale passing, from some unknown northern region, southward to more genial climes. We talked of fixed ice, yet in one day twelve miles of it came away, and nearly beset us amongst its fragments. We heard Captain Penny's report that there was water to be seen north of the remaining belt, of about ten miles in width. We were like deaf adders; we were obstinate, and went into winter quarters under Griffith's Island, believing that nothing more could be done, because a barrier of fixed ice extended across Wellington Channel! We were miserably mistaken.

The expedition under Lieutenant De Haven was then drifting slowly over the place where we, in our ignorance, had placed fixed ice in our charts; and to them likewise the wisdom of an all-merciful Providence revealed the fact of a northern sea of open water, that they might be additional witnesses in the hour of need. We cannot do better than read the plain unvarnished tale of the gallant American—a tale of calm heroism under no ordinary trials, which stamps the document as the truthful narration of a gentleman and a sailor. He says, after describing the being beset by young ice in the mouth of Wellington Channel, and drifting northward, owing to southerly winds,—

"On the 18th September we were above Cape Bowden. . . . . To account for this drift, the fixed ice of Wellington Channel, which we had observed in passing to the *westward*, must have been broken up, and driven to the southward by the heavy gale the 12th (September).

"We continued to drift slowly to the N. N. W. until the

22d, when our progress appeared to be arrested by a small low island, which was discovered about seven miles distant.

"*Between Cornwallis Island and some distant high land visible in the north, appeared a wide channel, leading to the westward.* A dark, misty-looking cloud which hung over it (technically termed frost-smoke) was indicative of much open water in that direction.

"Nor was the open water the only indication that presented itself in confirmation of theoretical conjecture as to a milder climate in that direction. As we entered Wellington Channel the signs of animal life became more abundant."

So much, then, for the barrier of ice in Wellington Channel in 1850. Let us now speak of what was there in 1851. On the 11th of August about as much fixed floe was remaining in Wellington Channel as had been found by us on the previous year, *a month later in the season.* On that occasion, late as it was, we have the evidence of Lieutenant De Haven to prove the channel opened: why should we doubt it doing so in 1851? An open sea existed on both sides of a belt of ice, rotten, full of holes, unfit to travel over (as Penny's officers reported it), full thirty days before the winter set in; is there an Arctic navigator hardy enough to say he believes that that belt would have been found there on the next spring-tide after our squadron was liberated from Griffith's Island? Then, I repeat, if it is allowed that Wellington Channel was open in 1819, 1820, 1850, and 1851, it is natural to infer that it was open when Franklin wished to pass through it in 1846, and that, under such circumstances, he would, in obedience to his orders, have gone by it to the N.W.

The day has not long passed by when it was tried to be proved, on *undoubted testimony*, that Barrow's Strait was barred with the accumulated ice of years,—and this in the face of an autumnal drift of a naval squadron for 350 miles in the pack of Lancaster. What say these barrier-builders to the winter drift of the American schooners under Lieutenant De Haven? Does his marvellous cruise teach us nothing? Between the 1st of November, 1850, and the 6th of June, 1851, his squadron was swept in one vast field of ice from the upper part of Wellington Channel to the southward of Cape Walsingham, in Davis's Straits, through a tortuous route of full 1000 miles! Yes, reader, the "Rescue" and "Advance" were beset in young bay-ice in and about Wellington Channel; but during the winter, amidst the darkness, amidst fierce gales, when the God of storms alone could and did shield those brave barks, they and *the ice* in *which they had been beset*, moved, with few pauses, steadily and slowly to the Atlantic Ocean, and reached it by the summer of the following year.

It is true, our expedition was prevented, by ice, from advancing to the west of Griffith's Island. But let it not be supposed that we came, in that direction, upon any *fixed* bar of ice or interminable floe-edge: far otherwise; for when, as I have elsewhere said, Lieutenant Aldrich was sent, a few days after our arrival at winter quarters, to travel on foot to Lowther Island, he found the task a hopeless one, as *water*, bay-ice, and a broken pack, lay between Somerville Island and it. We, likewise, in our spring journeys, found ice, smooth as glass, formed, evidently during the past winter, surrounding Lowther Island. It was traced by Lieutenant M'Clintock, leading, in exactly the form of the lead of water found in 1819 and 1820 by Sir E. Parry, in his voyage to Winter Island; and there can be little doubt, that, beyond the floe-pieces which choked the channel between Griffith's Island and Cape Bunny, we should, in 1850, have found water leading us to Winter Harbour, and up the noble channel north of Byam Martin Island.

Enough of icy barriers. I do not believe in Nature having placed such fixtures on the "vasty deep;" but I am ready to allow that there are places in which accumulations of ice naturally exist, and where the ice moves away less rapidly than in other parts. By looking at the chart, and taking into consideration the geographical conformation of such spots, the cause will at once appear.

In a line across the head of Davis's Straits, the pack hangs, because it is there met, in its downward course, by the whole weight of the Atlantic Sea, and strong southerly gales blowing up that funnel-shaped strait. About Leopold Island the pack hangs, for it is acted upon by the cross-tides of Wellington Channel and Regent's Inlet running athwart those of Barrow's Strait, and forming a sort of eddy, or still water. This occurs again in the *elbow* of Wellington Channel, and between Griffith's Island and Cape Bunny, where a narrowing strait, and the cross-tide of the channel towards the American coast, tie up the broad floes formed in the great water-space west of that point; and lastly, a similar choke takes place, apparently off the S. W. extreme of Melville Island.

Failing in barriers, these Job's comforters dismiss the subject by swallowing up the "Erebus" and "Terror," hull, masts, sails, and crew, in some especially infernal tempest or convulsion executed for the occasion: they—the Job's comforters—have no similar case to adduce in proof of such a catastrophe. Every body who goes to the frozen regions tells of the hairbreadth escapes and imminent dangers attendant on Arctic navigation. I am free to acknowledge, I have "piled the agony" to make my work sell. Behold the "Pioneer" in a nip in Melville Bay; the "Resolute" thumping the pack off Griffith's Island; the "Assistance" holding on to a floe-edge with a moving one threatening to sink her; and the "Intrepid" on the slope of an iceberg, high and dry: yet all are safe and sound in Woolwich dockyard: the brigs, "Rescue" and "Advance," beset for 267 days, drifting during a Polar winter 1150 miles, enduring all possible hardship and risk, yet both vessels and men are safe and sound. Captain Penny's two vessels, the "Lady Franklin" and "Sophia," if their figure-heads could speak, would "a tale unfold." Not the most extraordinary part of their adventures was, being caught in a gale in a bay on the coast of Greenland, and being forced by a moving iceberg through a field of ice full three feet thick, the vessels rearing and plunging through it; yet they are all safe and sound. The "North Star," the "Enterprise," and "Investigator," and farther back, the "Terror," farther still, the "Dorothea" and "Trent," have, with many more we could enumerate, seen no ordinary Arctic dangers; but, thanks to a merciful Providence, unattended with loss of life. Why, therefore, in the name of charity, consign those who are dear to us, as relatives, friends, or countrymen, to sudden death in the dark waters of Lancaster Sound or Baffin's Bay. No one who knew the men of that gallant squadron would so libel the leader, or his officers, as to suppose them to have turned back when at the threshold of their labours: if he does so, he does them foul injustice. And against such I appeal, in the name of that humanity which was never invoked in vain in a Christian land.

Give the lost ones the benefit of the doubt, if there is one on your minds. Let not selfish indifference to your fellow-creatures' fate induce you to dismiss the question by adopting any of the horrible opinions to which unfeeling men have given utterance. True it is, they are in sad peril; true it is, they have suffered long and much; true it is, that many may have fallen by the way: but the remnant, however small, of that heroic band, be assured, by one who knew many of them intimately and dearly, will despair not, but, trusting in their God, their Queen, and country, they will cling to hope with life's latest breath.

They have done their duty: let us not be wanting in ours. The rescue of Franklin's squadron, or the solution of their fate, entails no extraordinary risk of life upon the part of those employed in the search. Insurances to any amount—and I speak from a knowledge of the fact—may be effected in the various insurance offices in London with a lighter premium than is demanded for the Bights of Benin or Bengal. This is a pretty good test, and a sound practical one, too, of the much-talked-of dangers of Polar navigation. Ships are often lost; but the very floe which by its pressure sinks the vessel saves the crew.

In short, we have every thing to stimulate Arctic exploration. No loss of life; (for Franklin it will be time enough to mourn when we know he is not of the living;) the wonderful proofs lately acquired of a Polar sea; the undoubted existence of animal life in regions which were previously supposed to be incapable of supporting animal life; the result of the deeply philosophical inquiries of the talented geographer, Mr. Peterman, which seem to establish the fact of an open Polar sea during the severest season of the year; and lastly, the existence of Esquimaux in a high northern latitude in Baffin's Bay, who appear to be so isolated, and so unconnected with their brethren of South Greenland, as to justify us in connecting them rather with the numerous ruined habitations found westward as far as Melville Island, and lead the mind to speculate upon some more northern region,—some *terra incognita*, yet to be visited by us,—encourages us, aye, urges us not to halt in our exploration. Humanity and science are united in the cause:

where one falters, let a love for the other encourage us to persevere.

Franklin and his matchless followers need no eulogy from me; the sufferings they must have undergone, the mystery that hangs over them, are on every tongue in every civilized land.

The blooming child lisps Franklin's name, as with glistening eye and greedy ear it hears of the wonders of the North, and the brave deeds there done. Youth's bosom glows with generous emotion to emulate the fame of him who has gone where none as yet have followed. And who amongst us does not feel his heart throb faster in recalling to recollection the calm heroism of the veteran leader, who, when about to enter the unknown regions of which Wellington Channel is the portal, addressed his crews in those solemn and emphatic words of Holy Writ,—his motto, doubtless,—"Choose ye this day whom you will serve;" and found in that blissful choice his strength and his endurance.

To rescue even one life were surely well worthy our best endeavours; but if it so please an all-merciful Providence that aid should reach Franklin's ships too late to save even that one, yet would we have fulfilled a high and imperative duty: and would it be no holy satisfaction to trace the last resting-place of those gallant spirits? to recover the records, there assuredly to be found, of their manly struggle, under hardships and difficulties, in achieving that North-west Passage, in the execution of which they had laid down their lives? and to bring back to their surviving relatives and friends those last kind messages of love, which show that sincere affection and stern sense of duty sprang from one source in their gallant and generous hearts?

Yes, of course it would. Then, and not till then—taking this, the gloomiest view of the subject—shall we have done our duty towards the captains, officers, and crews of Her Majesty's ships "Erebus" and "Terror;" and then, and not until then, of their honoured leader we may safely say:—

"His soul to Him who gave it rose;
God led its long repose,
Its glorious rest!
And though the warrior's sun has set,
Its light shall linger round us yet,
Bright, radiant, blest!"

THE END.

Made in United States
Troutdale, OR
08/30/2023

12501533R00141